# The Southern Journey
## of Alan Lomax

# The Southern Journey
## of Alan Lomax
### *Words, Photographs, and Music*

WITH AN ESSAY BY
**TOM PIAZZA**

INTRODUCTION BY WILLIAM R. FERRIS
MUSIC-CD INCLUDED

THE LIBRARY OF CONGRESS

IN ASSOCIATION WITH

W. W. NORTON & COMPANY
NEW YORK | LONDON

Library of Congress staff:
W. Ralph Eubanks, *Director of Publishing*
Aimee Hess Nash, *Writer/Editor*
Todd Harvey, *Curator*, Alan Lomax Collection,
    American Folklife Center

*Cover photo:* Bob Pratcher (with fiddle) and
    Miles Pratcher (with guitar) on Ed Young's
    porch, Como, MS, September 22 or 23, 1959.
*Back cover photo:* Wade Ward listening to
    playback with Alan Lomax at the Ward home,
    Galax, VA, August 29 to 31, 1959.
*Title page photo:* Ada Combs playing banjo
    for children on her porch, Whitesburg, KY,
    c. September 7, 1959.

**Library of Congress
Cataloging-in-Publication Data**
Lomax, Alan, 1915–2002, photographer.
The southern journey of Alan Lomax : words,
photographs, and music / with an essay by
Tom Piazza; introduction by William R. Ferris.
— 1st edition.
    pages    cm
Includes bibliographical references and
    discography.
ISBN 978-0-393-08107-7 (hardcover)

1. Folk musicians—Southern States
—Pictorial works.
2. Southern States—Pictorial works.
3. Southern States—Social life and customs
—20th century—Pictorial works.
4. Lomax, Alan, 1915–2002.
I. Piazza, Tom, 1955–  II. Title.
ML87.L66    2013
781.62'13075—dc23
        2012027150

W. W. Norton & Company
500 Fifth Avenue, New York, NY 10110
www.wwnorton.com
W. W. Norton & Company Ltd.
Castle House, 75/76 Wells Street, London,
    WIT 3QT

10  9  8  7  6  5  4  3  2  1

**LIBRARY OF CONGRESS**

# Contents

# Southern Journey Field Trip Itinerary

This itinerary was compiled from the sound recording containers and photographs made during the Southern Journey. These documents sometimes contained incomplete or contradictory information. In total, Alan Lomax made 798 black-and-white and color images between August 1959 and May 1960 in Alabama, Arkansas, Georgia, Kentucky, Mississippi, Tennessee, and Virginia. In 1959 he was assisted by Shirley Collins and in 1960 he was assisted by his daughter Anna Lomax.

## August 1959

8/24–25: Salem and Bluefield, VA
8/28–31: Hillsville, Rugby, and Galax, VA

## September 1959

9/3: Williamson, Chillhowie, and Saltville, VA
9/6: Blackey and Mayking, KY
c. 9/7: Whitesburg, KY
c. 9/8–11: Nashville, TN and Lexington, AL
9/12: Fyffe and Huntsville, AL
9/16–20: Parchman and Lambert, MS
9/20–26: Como, Harmontown, Independence, and Senatobia, MS
9/30: Tate County, MS and Memphis, TN

## October 1959

10/1: Hughes, AR
10/3–4: Memphis, TN
c. 10/5–7: Greers Ferry, AR
10/6: Timbo and Landis, AR
10/7–9: Eastern Arkansas
10/7–9: Parchman, MS
10/10: Livingston, AL
10/12: St. Simons Island, GA

## April 1960

4/4: Ark, VA
4/6: Weems or Whitestone, VA
c. 4/4–28: St. Simons Island, GA
4/25–27: Williamsburg, VA
4/30: Belleville, VA

## May 1960

5/1: Portsmouth, VA
5/3: Norfolk, VA
5/5: Weems, VA
5/6: Warrenton, VA

# *Acknowledgments*

The Library of Congress wishes to thank the following staff members for their significant contributions to this book: Todd Harvey, curator of the Alan Lomax Collection in the American Folklife Center, for his scholarship in preparing the itinerary, discography, bibliography, and captions; Aimee Hess Nash, writer/editor in the Publishing Office, for managing the project and contributing to the image selection and captions; Wilson McBee, former editorial assistant in the Publishing Office, who recognized the value of these photographs and came up with the original book proposal; Hicks Wogan, former editorial assistant in the Publishing Office, for his assistance with the captions and discography; Peggy Bulger, former director of the American Folklife Center, for her support of the project; and W. Ralph Eubanks, director of publishing, for nurturing the book from start to finish.

The Library would also like to thank Anna Lomax Wood, Don Fleming, and Nathan Salsburg of the Association of Cultural Equity for their permission to publish the photographs in this book, for contributing the selection of songs and track notes for the accompanying album, for reviewing the text, and for their willingness to share their knowledge and expertise; and the journal *Southern Cultures* of the University of North Carolina at Chapel Hill, which generously gave permission to reproduce Bill Ferris's piece "Alan Lomax: the Long Journey."

Finally, the Library thanks Jim Mairs, editor at W. W. Norton, whose vision helped shape the book; Austin O'Driscoll, editorial assistant at W. W. Norton, who helped facilitate its publication; and John Bernstein of John Bernstein Design Inc. for his elegant design of this volume.

# *Foreword*

During his lifetime, Alan Lomax changed the way Americans and much of the world listen to music. He was one of the twentieth century's most prolific and talented documentarians, as well as a singer, songwriter, broadcaster, and civil rights activist. His ethnomusicological theories are still debated in universities. Above all, he gave to posterity the most important folklife collection ever assembled and which now rests in the archives of the Library of Congress. If Alan were alive today he would still be hard at work collecting, analyzing, and promoting the music, art, and culture of the world's peoples.

In March of 2004, the American Folklife Center at the Library of Congress acquired the Alan Lomax Collection, which comprises the exceptional ethnographic films, recordings, photographs, manuscripts, and notes that Lomax amassed over six decades. The acquisition was made possible through a cooperative agreement between the American Folklife Center (AFC) and the Association for Cultural Equity (ACE) and supported by the generosity of an anonymous donor.

The Library of Congress was already home to the groundbreaking field recordings that Alan and his father, John A. Lomax, created during their tenure as archivists for the Archive of American Folk Song (1932–1942). Together and singly, the Lomaxes undertook a vast documentation of African American and Afro-Caribbean music encompassing the southern United States, the Bahamas, Haiti, and the eastern Caribbean, as well as extended musical biographies of Leadbelly, Vera Hall and her cousin Doc Reese, and Jelly Roll Morton. In 1936 the elder Lomax organized and edited the WPA's Slave Narrative project, now residing at the Library. The Lomaxes also surveyed the folk song traditions of the Ozarks and Appalachia, and of lumbermen, sailors, fishermen, bargemen, Native Americans, and European immigrants in the northern and midwestern states. Alan made the first recordings of Muddy Waters, Fred McDowell, and David "Honeyboy" Edwards. He facilitated the careers of Leadbelly, Woody Guthrie, Pete Seeger, Burl Ives, Josh White, Sonny

Terry and Brownie McGhee, Big Bill Broonzy, Shirley Collins, Wade Ward, Almeda Riddle, Hobart Smith, and many others. Once Alan left the employment of the Library, he continued to widen his scholarship and fieldwork for another fifty years. Established at Hunter College in New York City, Alan developed a collection that became an international resource much sought after by the world's music scholars. He and his daughter Anna organized the Association for Cultural Equity (ACE) to continue the work that he had begun and to ensure that his collections and research would be preserved and appreciated.

Together the American Folklife Center and ACE have presented the Alan Lomax Collection to the interested public at a national symposium, through award-winning recordings, in online presentations, through sponsorship of an Alan Lomax Fellowship at the Library's Kluge Center, and now through this groundbreaking book of his Southern images. We hope that this publication will help a new generation of readers to discover the richness of America's many-faceted heritage, for the Alan Lomax Collection belongs to all of us.

—Peggy A. Bulger, *Director*   —Anna Lomax Wood, *Executive Director*
  American Folklife Center    Association for Cultural Equity

*Alan Lomax listening to playback at the home of Wade Ward,*
*Galax, VA, August 31, 1959.*

# Alan Lomax:
# The Long Journey

## WILLIAM R. FERRIS

How can we wrap our arms around Alan Lomax? He was a force of nature who appeared superhuman. I thought of Alan as a Minotaur—half man, half supernatural—who defied life as we know it. His very walk seemed to defy gravity as he slid gracefully with his distinctive gait. Sally Yerkovich recalls seeing Alan one day at the National Endowment for the Arts as he and his sister Bess walked side by side down the hall, each holding reading glasses in their extended right hand. They moved with that familiar Lomax stride that covered great distances and led them both to people and places that we celebrate today.

No two institutions have shaped my life more deeply than Alan Lomax and the Library of Congress, and their worlds are inextricably linked. We should reflect on the appropriate symmetry of the Library of Congress's acquisition of Thomas Jefferson's library of 6,487 books in 1815 and of Alan Lomax's library of 5,000 hours of sound recordings, 400,000 feet of motion picture film, 2,450 videotapes, 2,000 scholarly books and journals, hundreds of photographic prints and negatives, and over 120 linear feet of manuscripts in 2004. Standing two centuries apart, Thomas Jefferson and Alan Lomax are both icons of American culture, and their legacy is intimately tied to this great library. Their respective collections are intellectual bookends that ground us both in our nation's past and in its future. Thomas Jefferson and Alan Lomax chronicled writ-

This essay was first presented as the keynote address in January 2006 at a conference titled "The Lomax Legacy: Folklore in a Globalizing Century," sponsored by the American Folklife Center and the Association for Cultural Equity, New York, at the Library of Congress in Washington, D.C. It later appeared in the fall 2007 volume of *Southern Cultures*, published by the University of North Carolina Press. This version has been adapted slightly.

ten and oral traditions that together constitute our cultural birthright as Americans. Mr. Jefferson would be proud to know that his library has grown to over 29 million books, and Alan must be wryly smiling to see old friends and colleagues gathered to honor his legacy.

Alan Lomax's passion for folk music is part of an American tradition that historian Bryan Garman links with Walt Whitman's celebration of the working-class hero. In *Leaves of Grass* Whitman dreamed of a race of singers who would celebrate the working class as the heart of American democracy. Garman argues that Whitman inspired musicians such as Woody Guthrie, Bob Dylan, and Bruce Springsteen, each of whom chronicles American song. Like these singers, Lomax had deep ties with twentieth-century American folksingers.

"There is an impulsive and romantic streak in my nature that I find difficult to control when I go song hunting," Alan Lomax confessed. His love for music and for poets like Carl Sandburg is reflected in the prose style of his writings on music and dance. Scorning what he called "chair-bound scholars," he pursued an unending journey in search of the truth and beauty that he found in folk song and dance.

The Library of Congress was a second home for both Alan Lomax and his father, John Lomax. They worked at the Library's Archive of Folk Song for many years, and each deposited thousands of recordings there. Their recordings of songs like "Rock Island Line," "Good Night, Irene," and "John Henry" are as familiar to Americans as our national anthem.

As a teenager Alan traveled with his father to prisons, lumber camps, and black communities throughout the South. After John Lomax's death on January 26, 1948, Alan continued his father's work as he recorded, filmed, and studied folk music throughout the South and around the world. Alan clearly saw this work as a monument to his father's life. The father and son shared a tough love that was forged by the worlds that shaped them in Texas.

The intimate relationship Alan shared with his father is paralleled by that of Pete Seeger and his father, Charles Seeger. The Lomaxes and Seegers are considered the "first families" of American folk music. Coming from starkly different backgrounds, they were drawn together by a shared love of the music of the American South. John Lomax wrote that his family moved in an ox-drawn wagon from Goodman, Mississippi, to

Texas in 1869. He declared that his family belonged to the "upper crust of the po' white trash." With deep roots in Mississippi and Texas, both John and Alan Lomax passionately collected the songs of their region.

The Seeger family had equally deep roots in New England. Pete Seeger recalls that he studied at "a little alternative school in Connecticut. I first started learning about…a place called the South. We sang…'Oh, Susannah, I come from Alabama with a banjo on my knee.' It was a distant, romantic place, like the Far West or the islands of the Caribbean. And I didn't think I'd ever go down there."

Pete's father, Charles Seeger, and stepmother, composer Ruth Crawford Seeger, were both musicologists, and she wrote musical notations for many of the songs that the Lomaxes published. In an interview I did with Charles Seeger, he described how he first met the Lomaxes when he and the composer Henry Cowell were asked by Macmillan Publishers

> to advise them on a manuscript that had come in from a man named Lomax.…
>
> Well they came in,…John and Alan, and the manuscript was there, and Alan was ready to punch either Henry or me in the face. "These goddamned expert musicians, they don't know anything about folk music. They don't know anything about music, anyway!"
>
> Well, Henry and I opened the things and said, "My God, these are marvelous songs." This was about '33 or '34. "These are perfectly marvelous songs, and the notations are terrible. There's practically nothing there that doesn't have mistakes, wrong clefs, wrong accidentals, and everything else," I said. "You've got to have these notations made over, and the book is going to be very successful." Well, it was *American Ballads and Folk Songs,* and it was published. Alan softened up a little bit towards the end, and we presently became very good friends. In fact, he became a member of the family.
>
> So when Peter became interested in playing the banjo and singing songs that were accompanied by the banjo, I sent him to study the recordings in the Library of Congress, which is about the best school that there is. In fact, it's the only "school" that I know of. You just go in there and listen to recordings, and after you get sufficiently saturated with them, you know something.

The Library of Congress played a central role in bringing the Lomaxes and the Seegers together through their shared love for southern music. Alan Lomax hired Pete Seeger for fifteen dollars a week to work at the Library of Congress to listen to their recordings. Pete Seeger recalls that Alan had a lot of youth and energy and the experience of working as his father's assistant for a number of years. I think within five years he did more than most other archivists had done in fifty years. He was a whirlwind of energy, and with no budget to speak of. He meets an actor named Burl Ives. He says, "Burl, why are you wasting your time being an actor. You should be giving concerts of folk songs…" He taught Burl "Blue Tail Fly." He says, "Take it lightly. Don't push it." Got the song out of the book. He went to a nightclub owner, Max Gordon, of the Village Vanguard. He says, "Here's Josh White. Why don't you have him sing at your nightclub?" And Josh had a very successful career as a nightclub performer. Alan started it off.

Stories about Alan Lomax and his exploits are legendary. Folksinger Joe Hickerson recalls that while doing research in the Library of Congress Music Division, Lomax was sitting at a table across from a student who was reading his book *Folk Songs of North America*. At one point the student looked across the table and asked, "Is Alan Lomax still alive?"

Lomax replied, "Just barely."

Today, Alan Lomax is very much alive. His legacy is ensured by the reissuing of *The Land Where the Blues Began* and the publication of *Alan Lomax: Selected Writings, 1934–1997*, edited by Ronald D. Cohen. Both of these books include a CD with selections of field recordings and lectures by Lomax. In addition, the reissuing of all the Lomax recordings by Rounder Records, the 2005 publication of *Jelly Roll Morton: The Complete Library of Congress Recordings by Alan Lomax* with John Szwed's essay "Doctor Jazz," and the acquisition of the Alan Lomax Collection by the Library of Congress assure us that Alan Lomax's legend will endure. The film *O Brother, Where Art Thou?* featured a recording Alan Lomax made in Parchman Penitentiary of James Carter and other inmates singing "Po' Lazarus." The work song captured the imagination of millions of viewers who saw the film and of over ten million listeners who purchased its soundtrack. The fiftieth anniversary of Lomax's Southern Journey trip in 2010 saw the publication of Szwed's comprehensive biography, *Alan Lomax: The Man Who Recorded the World,* and a five-volume LP set of Southern Journey recordings issued by Mississippi Records.

Throughout his life Lomax continued to return to Mississippi to document and study its worlds of music and race. His book *The Land Where the Blues Began* chronicles these journeys and the classic recordings that Lomax made with blues artists like Muddy Waters.

When Zora Neale Hurston met Alan Lomax in New York in 1935, she wrote his father John Lomax that Alan "told me how you used to take him in your arms when he was a small boy & restless and walk the sidewalks with him and sing to him and tell him tales."

Hurston and Alan Lomax became close friends and later made field recordings together in Florida. Both are remembered for their strong, enigmatic characters and for their memorable portraits of black folklore. Lomax called *Mules and Men* "the most engaging, genuine, and skillfully written book in the field of folklore."

In 1941–42 Lomax also collaborated with the pioneering black sociologist, Charles Spurgeon Johnson of Fisk University, whose work he greatly admired, and Johnson's students Lewis Wade Jones and Samuel C. Adams Jr. in researching the relationships between music and society in Coahoma County, Mississippi. John Work III, a noted composer and folklorist of the Fisk Music Department, was selected to create musical transcriptions of the material they collected.

Allison Davis, Burleigh Gardner, and Mary Gardner, an interracial team of sociologists, conducted research for their book *Deep South* (1941) in Natchez, Mississippi. They chose to work independently because of local racial attitudes. John Dollard's *Caste and Class in a Southern Town* (1937) and Hortense Powdermaker's *After Freedom* (1939) are sociological studies of the Mississippi Delta town of Indianola—B.B. King's home—and neither scholar mentions the blues. In stark contrast to these studies, Lomax, his wife, Elizabeth, and John Work moved as an interracial team within Delta communities.

No other folklorist in the twentieth century worked with black performers and academic colleagues as Alan Lomax did throughout his career. Zora Neale Hurston, John Work, Lewis Wade Jones, Samuel Adams, and Worth Long all collaborated with Lomax on major collecting projects in the American South. And no other folklorist honored the lives of black artists and their musical legacy through books, films, and recordings as did Alan Lomax. The artists with whom he worked include Jelly Roll Morton, Leadbelly, and Muddy Waters.

Throughout his career Alan Lomax was fascinated by the technology that he used to record songs. He and his father used a portable recording rig that weighed five hundred pounds and engraved a sound groove on aluminum discs. He later used a lighter machine that engraved acetate discs. Each new generation of recorders was lighter, recorded for longer periods, and captured better-quality sound. Lomax was clearly on a mission, and through his recorder he "gave a voice to the voiceless. It…put neglected cultures and silenced people into the communication chain."

If Lomax was fascinated by his recording rig, so were the blues artists whom he recorded. While some feared the machine, others saw it as a way to escape their oppressive worlds. Memphis bluesman Willie B. reassured other musicians that, "just like a cotton gin takes two, three

***James Carter chopping wood, Mississippi State Penitentiary, likely Camp B, Lambert, MS, September 19 or 20, 1959.***

Alan and his father had visited the Mississippi State Penitentiary several times before Alan returned there during his Southern Journey. Among the prisoners he documented was James Carter, who led a group singing "Po' Lazarus." This performance was included on Alan's 1960 LP *Bad Man Ballads*, and appeared later in the 2000 film *O Brother, Where Art Thou?* When the soundtrack began to sell millions of copies, eventually winning a Grammy, Mr. Carter became again a wanted man. The 76-year-old was located in Chicago, presented with a substantial royalty check, and flown to the Grammy Awards ceremony. James Carter died in 2003.

wagonloads of cotton and squeezes it down to just one bale so you can ship it where you want to go, this microphone squeezes me and my song down into that little wavery line and they can ship me out to wheresomever they want me to sing. See the mystery?"

Lomax had little interest in the writings of Richard Wright and William Faulkner, both of whom chronicled Mississippi Delta worlds and black southerners like those whose voices he recorded. Lomax argued that Wright despised the Mississippi working class, while "Faulkner scarcely gives the reader a hint at what black life or feelings are like. ... Did he ever hear music, such songs as are described in these pages?"

While Lomax recorded brilliant performances of blues artists in the Delta and within its dreaded world of Parchman Penitentiary, he was fascinated by fife and drum musicians whom he discovered in the hills around Senatobia, Mississippi. There, in 1942, he tracked down Sid Hemphill, a blind musician known as the "boar-hog musician of the hills." Hemphill sang and played guitar, fiddle, mandolin, snare drum, fife, bass drum, quills, banjo, and organ. He was acknowledged as the musical patriarch of his community. Ed Young, a younger musician from the same area, played the fife, and Lomax observed that, when he played, Young assumed the position of Pan, the Greek god of pleasure. "He always danced as he played, his feet sliding along flat to the ground to support his weaving pelvis, enticing someone in the crowd to cut it with him, turning this way and that, always with dragging feet and bent knees, and always leaning toward the earth."

Lomax understood that the fife and drum music he recorded linked Mississippi black music to its African roots. During slavery, drums were outlawed throughout the American South because whites associated them with the Haitian slave revolt led by Toussaint Louverture. Few black drumming traditions endure today outside the Mississippi hill country, and Lomax was struck by dances that accompanied the music. During one memorable dance, "the women pulled their skirts tight, tight around buttocks and thighs, and an old lady 'balled the jack,' rotating her hips and squatting lower and lower till her dress tail stirred the dust and everybody shouted for joy. As she wound smoothly back to her upright stance, her shadow looked like a big bird, rising up in the orange light of the kerosene lanterns."

Lomax repeatedly returned to Mississippi—in 1947, 1948, 1959, and 1978—to record black music and to search for his own roots within the state. While interviewing Sid Hemphill, Lomax discovered a link to his own grandfather. They were discussing the song "Emmaline Take Your Time," when Lomax asked him,

> "Where did you learn to play that?"

> "I learnt from a cousin down in Como forty, fifty years ago, when I was a little boy. His name was Jeems Lomax."

> "My grandfather was named James Lomax," I said in astonishment. "Where was your cousin from?"

> "Oh, he come from down round Quitman County."

> "That's where my grandfather lived before he went to Texas," I said.

> "Maybe you-all's related," said Blind Sid, beginning a laugh in which we all joined and which has lasted me until today.

Lomax's early recordings of black music—from Texas, Louisiana, Mississippi, and Tennessee in 1933, through Florida, Georgia, and the Bahamas in 1935, and his extensive 1937 Haitian field trip—and his recordings of Southern white music in Kentucky, Virginia, Arkansas, Georgia, Texas, etc., were the intellectual foundation for a career that spanned over sixty years. His later activities included fieldwork in the Upper Midwest, Ohio, New England, and New York; producing concerts for the Newport Folk Festival and the Roosevelt White House; radio broadcasting and record producing; writing books, plays, and articles; extensive recordings in the British Isles and Ireland, Spain, Italy, and the eastern Caribbean; and finally his Cantometrics and Choreometrics research. Among his early mentors and collaborators were Carl Sandburg, George Herzog, Archibald MacLeish, Zora Neale Hurston, Josh White, Huddie Ledbetter, Charles and Ruth Crawford Seeger, Jerome Wiesner, and Pete Seeger. And he inspired young folksingers like Pete Seeger and Bob Dylan in their musical careers.

In *Alan Lomax: Selected Writings, 1934–1997*, Ronald Cohen, Ed Kahn, Andrew Kaye, Matthew Barton, and Gage Averill organize Lomax's writings chronologically and provide helpful essays for each period in his sixty-year career. His earliest published work, "Sinful Songs of the Southern Negro," was published in *Southwest Review* in 1934 and foreshadows *The Land Where the Blues Began*. Gage Averill stresses that the disparate parts of Lomax's life—collecting, academic analysis, folklore revivalism, advocacy, and education—should be viewed as parts of a coherent whole that shaped one of the most complex creative minds of the twentieth century.

Building on over three decades of work, Lomax published "Folk Song Style" in *American Anthropologist* in 1959. In the article he called for a scientific approach to the world's music through the field of Cantometrics. "Using musical style analysis as a diagnostic instrument," he argued, "we can begin the study of the emotional and esthetic history of the world's people." Lomax later expanded this theory into his book *Folk Song Style and Culture*, which was published in 1968.

Having linked song and culture around the globe, Lomax then turned to dance and developed the field of Choreometrics. He used documentary film to study dance, just as he had used recordings to study song. Like his friend and colleague Margaret Mead, Lomax urged anthropologists and folklorists to film traditional dance throughout the world as part of their study.

Throughout his life, Alan Lomax worked passionately for civil rights and at times risked his life to collect the music he loved so deeply. In a letter to Guy Carawan that is included in the liner notes of the album *Freedom in the Air: A Documentary on Albany, Georgia, 1961–62*, Lomax wrote, "It must be wonderful to be with those kids who are so courageously changing the South forever. I hope they feel proud of the cultural heritage of their forebears. It was a heritage of protest against oppression, of assertion against hopelessness, of joy in life against death." Lomax equated his passion for civil rights with the need for "cultural equity." He argued that every nation should give "equal time" to their diverse cultures in broadcasting and in education. Lomax believed that most creative developments in art have "been the product of small communities … within larger entities."

He also understood the power of American culture and how it is transmitted globally. He argued passionately that "the standard Western European system of music education, taken to other cultural settings, is a form of aesthetic imperialism that is as destructive of native musical autonomy as the takeover of political and economic power is destructive of native initiative."

Such patterns of cultural imperialism also exist in America, he noted, pointing out that "ninety percent of the federal and local money spent on music goes to support one musical tradition—the symphonic, fine-arts tradition. ... Nowhere, for instance, does anyone teach the art of the American Negro spiritual, America's deep song."

Toward the end of his life, Alan Lomax was increasingly recognized as our nation's chronicler of American folk song. In 1986 he received the National Medal of the Arts from President Ronald Reagan. Today, Lomax's books, field recordings, and films are used in classrooms, museums, and libraries, as well as in films and television productions. His musical legacy touches every aspect of our culture.

Alan Lomax always reached out to the common man and woman and celebrated their lives. In a 1940 radio script he declared that "the essence of America lies not in the headlined heroes. ... but in the everyday folks who live and die unknown, yet leave their dreams as legacies."

While Alan Lomax made major contributions as a writer, scholar, and radio announcer, for me, his greatest contribution will always be his Southern recordings, particularly those from the Mississippi Delta. Far from the academy and the urban worlds where he lived most of his life, he renewed his spirit in those rural communities where on Saturday nights "the couples [were] glued together in a belly-to-belly, loin-to-loin embrace ... Slowly, with bent knees and with the whole shoe soles flat to the floor, they dragged their feet along its surface, emphasizing the off beat, so that the whole house vibrated like a drum. It was that sound we had heard a mile away in the moonlit night."

As an aspiring folklorist, Alan was my hero and mentor. While teaching at Yale in the seventies, I visited him at his home in New York and brought him to New Haven to speak to my students. It was his vision that inspired the work I later did at the University of Mississippi Center for the Study of Southern Culture. As I was leaving Yale in 1979, I wrote Alan that his spirit would be part of our center, and he responded, "I'd rather get in with both feet."

His vision also inspired my work at the National Endowment for the Humanities as we developed regional humanities centers and encyclopedias for states, cities, and regions throughout the nation. While at NEH, I met with Bess Lomax Hawes and Anna Lomax Wood to get their counsel on our plans and to send my greetings to Alan.

When I taught at Yale University in 1976, Alan wrote me a wonderful letter that in his characteristic voice was both critical and encouraging. "It seems to me that you are spread too thin and not digging deeply enough in the work you have collected or thinking hard enough about it. In my opinion, folklore is the hardest of all professions, and it takes a long time to make a good folklorist. I think you're well on your way and I know you've got to publish or perish, but I think it's a bad idea to settle for anything less than the best when what we do *does* count so much to the people, themselves. . . . I feel more than a friend—I feel that, in a way, I have been a sponsor of yours. . . . p.s. Bill, I guess this is an older man's letter to a younger colleague. . . . What I'm asking you to do, *no one* has done, but it must *be* done."

—William R. Ferris, University of North Carolina at Chapel Hill

*Alan Lomax with his camera at the 1979 Mississippi Delta Blues Festival in Greenville, MS.*

*Alan Lomax on Miles Pratcher's porch, Como, MS, September 22 or 23, 1959.*

# Alan Lomax:
# The Found World

## TOM PIAZZA

Amerian culture is nothing if not divided. Or say that it exists in a state of extraordinary tension within itself. It expands; its destiny is, or was, manifest. It moves forward; it grows. The United States began life as the New World, of course, and that designation still hangs over everything not just as a descriptive but as an injunction. Make it new. Get the latest version. Reinvent yourself.

But the winding and varied routes by which inhabitants came to be here, as well as the extraordinary variety of the landscape—Redwood forest to Gulf Stream waters, dismal swamp to amber waves of grain— seem to have wired a paradoxical undertow of nostalgia into the circuits. A fascination with the story of how you got to such a strange place, how you arrived. An endemic desire to bulldoze the past, linked to an obsession with memorializing that bulldozed past.

Those who came, those who stayed, kept pieces of the Old Country with them, songs, stories, ways of speaking, magic rocks and trails of crumbs leading back into an intelligible past, lights by which to read some kind of narrative into the disjunctive reality in which one had landed. Despite every imperative to lay aside one's Old World prejudices, get rid of one's accent, sign on to a culture that represented a radical break with the past, the psychic upheaval was too much to navigate cold. One needed some constellation by which to reckon one's position.

Against the forces of standardization and—the word is almost forced upon us—progress, were arrayed the ancient ballad, the familiar dance step, instrumental or vocal timbres that conveyed something beneath and beyond the level of strictly verbal language. Yet even these began to change their nature when unwrapped and exposed to the new air, and to the other modes of expression carried and unwrapped by other strangers. And that conversation—among English and Scottish and Irish ballads and African rhythms and tonal manipulation, German and Italian brass bands and marches, salon music, parlor songs, English music hall ditties and Hispanic and Caribbean dance rhythms—formed the template of an American musical culture that was not a mere withered limb of Europe's but something wholly new.

Of course these forms quickly became commercially exploited, through minstrelsy and traveling shows and, slightly later, vaudeville. And that commercial exploitation brought new air into previously protected pockets of the country as well as bringing local forms of expression into ever more immediate contact with a broader audience. This was either a curse or a blessing (or both) depending on your perspective. Either way, that process of mixing things up, which was so integral to the dynamism of American culture, was sure to threaten some aspect of the fabric of the old, closely held magic. That threat, to the extent that it was a threat, began to increase exponentially with the explosion of film, sound recording, and, slightly later, radio in the early decades of the twentieth century. In the minds of some, an alarm bell went off. If any of the old magic were to be preserved, even if only in memory, one might need to use the new technology to preserve it, before the new technology itself hurled it all into the irretrievable past.

There is always something mysterious about our affinities, even when they appear most explainable. If anyone's background ever seemed to prepare them to become the person they became, Alan Lomax's did. The greatest folklorist of the twentieth century, and perhaps of all time, was the son of a father, John A. Lomax, who was himself a pioneering collector of songs. Alan Lomax had been born into a historical moment in which new techniques for collecting and documenting folklore were making themselves available at a dizzying rate. And yet the energy with which he pursued the collection of folk expression, the insatiable appetite he had for the full variety of available material, the persistence with which he traveled and documented and proselytized is mysterious and, finally, inspiring of awe.

Alan Lomax is best known for his prodigious documentation of vernacular folk music through sound recordings. He started by accompanying his father through Southern penitentiaries in the early 1930s to

## Wayne Perry (with fiddle), Crowley, LA, June 1934.

In Baton Rouge, Louisiana, in 1933, John A. Lomax made the Library's first ethnographic disc recordings. As he described it in the 1933 *Report of the Librarian of Congress*: "…I received about July 15 a late model of one of the best types of portable recording machine. This machine, weighing 315 pounds, provided with Edison batteries, a rotary converter, amplifiers, a double-button carbon microphone, a dynamic speaker, and cutting and reproducing heads, I thenceforward carried in the rear of my Ford sedan." Throughout the 1930s and early 1940s the elder Lomax made annual collecting trips between Washington and Dallas. Invariably he stopped in Louisiana to document its exceptionally varied musical traditions, from Cajun waltzes to Anglo fiddle tunes, such as those played by Wayne Perry, and from ballads performed by African American minstrels to topical communal prison work songs.

24

***Mexican girls,***
***San Antonio, Texas,***
***1933–1934.***

This image was made during
John A. Lomax and Alan Lomax's
Library-sponsored field trip to
San Antonio, Texas, in May 1934.
The girls were hastily gathered
from the neighborhood by
Josephine Gonzalez (probably at
the center of the photograph).
They sang five songs that were
issued, a decade later, on the
Library's recording *Ethnic Music
of French Louisiana, the Spanish
Southwest, and the Bahamas.*
The photograph and recording
represent an interest in children's
folklore, and demonstrate a com-
mitment by the Library of Congress
to document the different ethnici-
ties comprising the American
patchwork. Alan's ideas, formu-
lated through decades of fieldwork,
would later be expressed in his
article "Appeal for Cultural Equity"
(1972) where he suggested that
"A grey-out is in progress which, if
it continues unchecked, will fill
our human skies with smog of the
phony and cut the families of men
off from a vision of their own cultural constellations."

record prisoners singing work songs. Slightly later he began making his own trips, through the Appalachians, Louisiana, the Midwest, and other locales where he recorded ancient ballads from the British Isles, blues, Cajun and Creole music, and more. He greatly expanded the Library of Congress's Archive of American Folk Song while working there in the late 1930s and early 1940s. In 1938 he recorded the reminiscences of New Orleans pianist and composer Jelly Roll Morton, who was then living in Washington, D.C.—a priceless record not only of the early years of jazz music but of the picaresque life of a restless American spirit as it cut across geographic and cultural lines. (*Mister Jelly Roll*, the book that Lomax stitched together out of those and other recordings, was a best seller on publication, and it remains in print, and widely read, today.) Lomax recorded both Leadbelly and Woody Guthrie for the Library of Congress and, on a 1941 collecting trip to Mississippi along with folklorist John Work, made the first recordings of the man who would later become famous as Muddy Waters.

He also produced widely disseminated and influential radio programs on folk music, recorded an astonishing spectrum of music in Europe throughout the 1950s, and continued all of these activities well into his eighth decade and the final years of the century, before his death in 2002, at age eighty-seven. He approached his mission with an acquisitive zeal that was, in itself, very American. He annexed huge tracts of world culture and claimed them for the flag of Folk Expression. His ambition was titanic, as was his achievement, and yet also profoundly paradoxical—full of reverence for the undefiled expression and yet strongly inflected by an ideological stance that inevitably marked his writing and theorizing about the materials.

With this stunning book of photographs, most of which were taken during a two-month period in 1959, on a collecting trip that has come to be called his "Southern Journey," we get a new window into that ambition and that paradox, along with a sometimes startlingly immediate view of the people who were the source of all that extraordinary musical expression. It offers a double vision, one that not only takes in Lomax's subjects and their context but reveals a side of Lomax himself, a vision hitherto available only in hints and glimpses.

**Uncle Rich Brown and John A. Lomax (left) at the home of Mrs. Julia Killingsworth, near Sumterville, AL, October 1940.**

John A. Lomax was honorary curator of the Archive of American Folk-Song (1932–1942) but spent much of his time away from Washington, often in the field. Sumter County, Alabama, which lies along the southwest border of the state, proved to be one of Lomax's most fertile collecting locations. During sessions in 1937 and 1940, at the behest of Mrs. Ruby Pickens Tartt of the Alabama Federal Writers' Project, Lomax recorded Rich Brown singing songs, many of them spirituals.

## 2.

Alan Lomax was born on January 31, 1915, in Austin, Texas. His father, John A. Lomax, already had a reputation as a collector of folk materials, most especially cowboy songs. His book *Cowboy Songs and Other Frontier Ballads* had been published five years earlier, with an introduction by President Theodore Roosevelt, no less. The elder Lomax was a force of nature. He had blown through his undergraduate years at the University of Texas in two years, and had subsequently spent a year studying at Harvard, partly under the tutelage of literature scholar and ballad expert George Lyman Kittredge, who was himself a student of Francis James Child, who assembled the epochal ten-volume collection *The English and Scottish Popular Ballads*.

Academic agreement on the significance of these materials was by no means unanimous, and Lomax Sr. never held a steady academic position as a professor. He had to piece together a living from twigs and scraps; he served as registrar and, later, secretary of the faculty and alumni association at the University of Texas; he taught English briefly at Texas A&M and he sold bonds in Chicago and, later, in Dallas, as well as constantly applying for grants and graduate fellowships. He also made a significant part of his living by traveling and giving lectures about cowboy songs. Self-dramatizing and even Barnumesque, he often performed the songs he collected and contextualized them with stories that cast the collecting of the songs as a romantic adventure in itself. Much the same would be true of his son.

Alan Lomax was sickly as a boy, and he was by all reports something of an intellectual prodigy. He attended private schools, first in Austin and then, for his senior year, at Choate. Although his father badly wanted Alan to attend Harvard, the young man elected instead to spend his freshman year at the University of Texas, in Austin, so that he could be near his ailing mother in Dallas. When she died, in May 1931, he was profoundly depressed and disoriented, but he agreed to go off to Harvard that fall.

Despite Alan's undisputed intelligence and energy, Harvard was not a good fit. Given the death of his mother, his early tastes of nightlife in the black sections of Austin, and his fledgling interest in radical political ideology, Cambridge was bound to seem claustral to him. He disliked the "sheltered Harvard students and the doubly-sheltered Harvard professors," as he described them in one letter home, and as the year went on his interest in his studies waned. He seems also to have begun to identify with the Communist movement, which at the time attracted so many idealistic younger Americans. At the end of that school year his scholarships were not renewed, and Alan decided to head back to Texas. He longed to join the Merchant Marine, to travel; in that same letter home he expressed admiration for a Russian movie he had seen, in which the characters were "working intensely, unselfconsciously, eating, drinking, anything, working with an enormous gusto that will probably always be denied to me." This combination of romantic energy with a genuine affinity for working-class people, along with a profound sense of the gulf between them and himself, would characterize Alan personally and professionally for the rest of his life.

Alan returned to the University of Texas for the 1932–33 school year. While he had been away, the nation's economic crisis had deepened, and John A. Lomax's bond business was doing badly. Alan sensed that his father was edging toward a deep and perhaps dangerous personal depression. John's song collecting activities had languished, and Alan began to encourage his father to resume them. He even proposed that they make a collecting trip together. And in the summer of 1933 they did just that, traveling south with newly acquired recording equipment, headed for a series of penitentiaries in order to collect work songs and field hollers from the prisoners. The trip marked John's return to active collecting and the beginning of Alan's life work.

*"Lightnin'" Washington, inmate, and group, Darrington State Prison Farm, Sandy Point, TX, April 1934.*

Home in Texas for the winter of 1933–1934, and with the Library's new disc recorder in hand, John A. Lomax visited several area prisons. At Sandy Point's Darrington State Prison Farm, Lomax recorded "Lightnin'" Washington leading a group of convicts singing communal work songs, including "Long John," "Hammer Ring," and "Go Down, Old Hannah," which became a 1960s folk revival standard. He wrote that "Negro songs in much of their primitive purity can be obtained probably as nowhere else from Negro prisoners in State and Federal penitentiaries. Here the Negroes are completely segregated and … have not yet been influenced by jazz and the radio." More analytically, he continued, "It is only by making field recordings of the singing of southern Negroes that the tonal, rhythmic, and melodic characteristics of Afro-American folk music can be accurately preserved."

# 3.

Today, with YouTube and Skype and camera phones, it is so easy to record and instantly transmit both audio and video information that it may be difficult to imagine the logistical challenge involved in the Lomaxes' early collecting efforts. When father and son headed south in the summer of 1933, they acquired a new machine that recorded directly onto discs that could be played back on an ordinary turntable. The disc recorder weighed over three hundred pounds, and it took up most of the rear of the car in which they traveled. Along with the recorder itself, they needed to carry piles of the aluminum blank discs that would contain the music. When it was impossible to get their portable-recording-studio-cum-car in proximity to the subject, Alan would have to remove the machine from the car and drag it to where the music was. Moreover, they did this during the heart of summer in the American South, in places where the temperatures regularly got into the 90s, or higher, and there was no air-conditioning—especially in the Texas, Louisiana, and Mississippi penitentiaries that were their primary destinations.

For Alan, the trip was a profound, life-changing experience. In remarks delivered in 1989 at the New York Public Library, he identified that trip as the occasion when he heard the music that first "allied me with the people, which made me forget Beethoven and all that...in the Texas prison camp, where black men, driven 'from can't to can't' under the shotgun had the glorious humanity to make great music." It was a shock to see men who might otherwise have been faceless and voiceless to outsiders show a sense of life and humor and wit, not to mention the will to beauty, in circumstances that were, to say the least, oppressive. It was that juxtaposition, of the painful human situation with the insistence on the assertion of humanity, that put not just a human face but a spiritual significance on a social dynamic that Alan had previously considered only in hypothetical terms.

The music itself, the songs, all were suddenly folded into a unified field of sorts. Rhythm, attitude, tone became connected to a body of physical gesture, stance, context that illumined everything with a light from a new angle. For Alan, it represented, in effect, a kind of secondary radicalization, the fusion of his political stance with the mission of collecting.

*James "Iron Head"
Baker, inmate,
Sugarland Prison
Farm, Sugarland, TX,
June 1934.*

James "Iron Head" Baker was
convict #3610 at Central State
Farm No. 1 in Sugarland, Texas.
A 63-year-old native of Dallas, he
called himself an "H.B.C. — habit-
ual criminal" and was in prison
for the sixth time for "porch-climb-
ing," or burglarizing homes. After
meeting and recording Baker in
1933, John A. Lomax wrote to
his soon-to-be second wife, Ruby
Terrill, that he had met a "black
Homer." A few years later he
secured a four-month furlough for
"Iron Head" from Governor James
Allred. The elder Lomax brought
"Iron Head" to other prisons
where, as he described it, he "used
this man to sing for the Negro
prisoners to show them the type
of songs I was collecting."

He apparently argued with his father about this connection for the
entire summer. John A. Lomax was never aligned with his son's radical
sympathies, nor with his racial sympathies. On more than one occasion
they had bitter, and sometimes public, arguments about the situation of
blacks in the South. Years later, after a 1940 concert of "Negro Folk Song
with Commentary," held at the Library of Congress, during which Alan
remarked pointedly from the stage about the mistreatment of Southern
blacks, Pete Seeger remembers John shouting that his son had "disgraced
the South."

Leftist politics had swerved in a new direction in the mid-1930s,
as historian Sean Wilentz points out brilliantly in his book *Bob Dylan
in America*. Earlier efforts to establish a "proletarian music" composed
by American composers trained in European classical technique were

replaced by a movement to use vernacular forms of music and culture to further the left-leaning ideological agenda. The "Popular Front" idea provided the ligature to connect the expressive efforts of "common people" with the ideals of a vanguard movement. What might have been seen in a different light as regressive, provincial, and backward had had its polarities reversed and now represented the voice of the folk, undefiled by the corrupting effects of commercial media and the temptations of big-city sophistication. So when Alan, who already had his sympathies pointed leftward, encountered not just the cultural expression of these prisoners but also the prisoners themselves, it had the effect of revelation.

In the summer of 1934, father and son made another Southern collecting trip together, during which they reunited with the most impor-

*African American children playing singing games, Eatonville, FL, 1935.*

Alan photographed these African American children's game songs and dances—an undercurrent existing in many of his field trips—perhaps at the behest of anthropologist Zora Neale Hurston (seen on the right in this photograph), whose presence created access to African American communities in Georgia and Florida during their 1935 field trip. Alan's interest in children's folklore was manifested in publication by his book *Brown Girl in the Ring* (1997), edited with J. D. Elder and Bess Lomax Hawes, and drawn primarily from Alan's 1962 trip to the eastern Caribbean. This interest is visible in images of the Hemphill children playing in Senatobia, Mississippi, on the Southern Journey.

tant discovery they had made the previous year, the songster and guitarist (and convicted murderer) Huddie Ledbetter, who would come to be known throughout the world as Leadbelly. Ledbetter was coming up for parole at the notorious Louisiana prison farm Angola, and a month after the Lomaxes' visit he was released. Leadbelly became John's driver and valet; John and Alan collaborated on a book of Leadbelly's songs. Although Alan inevitably had a relationship with Ledbetter, the singer's primary relationship, professional and personal, was with his father.

John A. Lomax was a huge figure, a dominating personality, and Alan both idolized him and felt overwhelmed and overshadowed by him. Twenty years later, during the eight years Alan spent in Europe, dodging the Red Scare that threatened his livelihood and his freedom back home, Alan wrote to his friend John Faulk that he had "at last almost emerged completely from my father's shadow, which I now realize always hung over me in America." This remark might be surprising to us now, given how much important work Alan had already accomplished by that point in his life, and yet it was a psychic fact for him. Early on, Alan attempted to get his own footing in the world as a folklorist, and he pursued that mission with an energy that must have been fueled, at least in part, by the need to push back against his father's huge influence.

In 1935 Alan made his first collecting trip without his father, through Georgia, Florida, and the Caribbean, in the company of the folklorists Mary Barnicle and Zora Neale Hurston. His activities soon began to eclipse his father's, in scope and magnitude. The following year, Alan began working at and for the Library of Congress. Between 1935 and 1942 he made collecting trips almost every year, covering an astonishing amount of territory, almost all of it east of the Mississippi River. In 1938 and 1939 his efforts centered on the Midwest and New England, respectively; the rest of the time his efforts led him south.

**Man posing holding a drum, Cat Island, Bahamas, July 1935.**

Alan made four field trips to the Caribbean: the Bahamas (1935); Haiti (1936–1937); the eastern Caribbean (1962); and St. Eustace and the Dominican Republic (1967). During the 1935 trip Alan noted to his Library of Congress colleagues his belief that Afro-Caribbean musical genres exhibited African roots more clearly than their American counterparts. Of his 1962 fieldwork he reflected, "Everywhere I found tidal pools and freshets of indigenous music and dance styles reflecting both the particular qualities of local life and the mainstream Creole performance style that plainly stemmed from West Africa." This impetus to understand and describe the complex mechanisms of acculturation led to his performance-style research of the 1950s through the 1990s.

During this time, and through the 1940s, Alan also produced radio shows and oversaw the assembling of several books, a couple in collaboration with his father. He was also increasingly involved in radical political activities, including Henry Wallace's presidential effort, and the formation, with Pete Seeger, of People's Songs, a project to harness the singing ideal to the labor movement by means of creating union choruses and gathering folk performers to raise money for progressive causes. In his foreword to *The People's Songbook*, published in 1948, Lomax wrote that the songs in the book were part of "an emerging tradition that represented a new kind of human being, a new folk community composed of progressives and anti-fascists and union members," and had been "tested in the fire of the people's struggle all around the world."

This kind of talk, unsurprisingly, put him on the radar of the FBI and other hunters of radicals. As early as 1942, he was questioned about his activities, under oath, by the FBI. Although he denied membership in the Communist Party, his activities pointed toward at least a degree of sympathy with radical movements. Although he was supported by Librarian of Congress Archibald MacLeish, and agency director J. Edgar Hoover declined to proceed with any action against him, Alan was to be watched closely from then on. For the rest of the 1940s he raised money for leftist causes, consorted with the likes of Paul Robeson, Earl Robinson

***Alan Lomax (left) and youngster on board boat, during recording expedition, Bahamas, 1935.***

Alan was twenty years old when he traveled to the Bahamas in 1935, the last leg of a field trip to Georgia and Florida made with Zora Neale Hurston and folklorist Mary Elizabeth Barnicle. Barnicle and Lomax heard Bahamian fire dancers in Florida and decided to continue on to the islands without Hurston. In a letter to his Library of Congress colleagues, Alan noted

that they soon were "bewitched by these fairy islands and busy recording the livest and most varied folk-culture we had yet run into." By 1935 Alan was already a veteran field worker, having spent portions of the previous two years as his father's companion and driver while they combed the South for vernacular American song.

Alan worked in radio from 1939 to 1957, relentlessly promoting vernacular music from the United States and around the world. His *Folk Music of America* series, part of the CBS American School of the Air, was an educational program intended for school children as well as adults. The January 9, 1940, episode, titled "Square Dances," featured the Bogtrotters from Galax, Virginia. Alan later visited one of the Bogtrotters, Wade Ward, on his Southern Journey trip. This photograph comes from group and individual portraits created by a CBS photographer sent to Galax to capture the Bogtrotters as they enjoyed the national broadcast of their prerecorded performance.

(who wrote the song "Joe Hill"), and Aaron Copland, and advocated for the cultural centrality of disadvantaged and working-class people. When the nation's fear of Russian-inspired communist infiltration began to come to a boil in the late 1940s, these activities were flags to attract the attention of red hunters and red baiters. When Lomax found himself listed, in June 1950, as a subversive in the pamphlet *Red Channels*, a listing of supposed communists and sympathizers in the media, Alan saw the writing on the wall. He left the United States in September 1950, ostensibly to assemble a library of world folk music for Columbia Records, and he stayed away for eight years.

*Alan Lomax (holding microphone) and Hamish Henderson (wearing glasses), Edinburgh, Scotland, 1958.*

Alan's output during his eight years in Europe is impressive. He created dozens of radio programs for the BBC, authored various articles, and compiled the book *The Folk Songs of North America* as well as several multivolume LP sets. Additionally, Alan made significant field excursions to the British Isles (1951–1953), Spain (1952–1953), and Italy (1954–1955). Collaboration with his European counterparts and the sheer extent of his time in the field honed Alan's skills as an ethnographer, an aptitude he would apply when he returned to the United States and began his Southern Journey.

# 4.

When Lomax left the country in 1950, he left his wife and child, his job, and the culture that had given him an overarching mythos, and which had been the topic, in a sense, of his work. What this self-imposed exile asked of him was that he extend the assumptions of his work at home and become a citizen of the world, or of the world's cultures, at least.

This he did brilliantly. Unencumbered by the methodology of traditional ethnologists and anthropologists, he traveled throughout the British Isles, as well as Spain and Italy, using some of the same techniques that he had employed at home to find traditional musicians and record them. He covered an astonishing amount of ground and, as he had done in the United States, captured music that would certainly not have been preserved in any other way.

It was also a period of great personal challenge and growth for Lomax. For a long time, he seems to have had questions about the nature of his involvement in his work, as well as his relation to his father and to the personal relationships in his life. He had been in psychoanalysis for

several years before he left the country. And yet there was a tension between his private search for meaning as an individual and the ideological rationale for his work: the idea that we are less important as individuals than as "links in a chain," in Pete Seeger's phrase. In the 1950s he would write that "the primary function of music is to remind the listener that he belongs to one certain part of the human race, comes from a certain region, belongs to a certain generation." The emphasis was not, in other words, on self-expression, or the realization of a personal vision of existence, but on ligature with the community, and with the past.

In an unsourced 1946 document quoted in John Szwed's biography of Lomax, *Alan Lomax: The Man Who Recorded the World*, Lomax himself addressed this disconnect between his underlying motives and the rationale for the work that came out of them. "What were my *own* purposes in living this way? What are my reasons for continuing to immerse myself in this quagmire of folklore?...What do I like? What do I think about? Why am I born? What path shall my feet follow? All the paths that have opened up before me so far have been the paths of other people...I know the kind of intellectual, moral and emotional structure that can be made out of folklore. It is a lack of *personal* conviction that is my problem."

**Alan Lomax with roll of film and unidentified man, Albarracín, Spain, October 15, 1952.**

Alan Lomax immigrated to London and Paris in 1950, ostensibly to undertake a massive recording project, the *Columbia World Library of Folk and Primitive Music*. His political views, however, had led to FBI investigation beginning in 1939 and blacklisting in the publication *Red Channels* in 1950. Alan found that a bohemian existence in Europe was preferable to dwindling professional opportunities in the U.S.

Alan's time in Europe, although he experienced homesickness, periods of frustration, and constant financial worries, had a transformative effect on him. Freed both from his father's "shadow" and from the harness of institutional involvement, he seemed to find his way toward a kind of pleasure and physical presence in the world, as well as a more direct, immediate connection to the people who made the music he recorded, which had eluded him before. Spain, in particular, seemed to open him up. In his notebook, he wrote, "Day hot. The sea near. Figs, oranges, plums, pears ripening... I decide to settle for life in every town and marry every sweet young *señorita* I see. Words, movement, ambition are conquered in the Balearics by the sheer pleasure of living... What I want to do is swim, sleep, stare, chat. And if there is anything more pleasant than chatting with a black-eyed girl on the *Rambla*, the shaded promenade in Palma, between 9 and 11:30 I never ran into it."

Perhaps not coincidentally, Alan began taking photos in earnest during his time in Europe. He had always taken pictures, but now he seemed more attuned than ever to the nuances of movement and expression that accompanied the musical performances he was documenting. He also began developing some of the theories about the relations between a region's sexual and social mores and the kinds of music produced by the region's people that later became codified in the theory he called "Cantometrics." His mind was full of plans—for books, for plays, for a television series, even for a ballet. "All the imaginative qualities that were repressed all my life are beginning to merge now for the first time. I can tackle literally anything I choose..." he wrote in a 1953 letter to his wife.

The great paradox is that even as he was being opened up in a new way to the life of the body and the senses, his analytical ambitions were shifting into overdrive. It was not enough to have the experiences and document the musical expression—he needed to evolve a theory of it all. Why these two famously antagonistic impulses—the experiential and the analytical—should have surged in him simultaneously with such vigor is anyone's guess. Was the analytic there to act as an instinctive brake on the flood of emotion and empathy? Did he need some justification for the vivid experiences he was having?

We can't know. What we do know is that during this time Alan was making plans for a kind of grand Wagnerian synthesis of psychology, anthropology, musicology, folklore, and technology to study, in biographer Szwed's words, "patterns of muscular tension in the body during singing, patterns of breathing in songs, variations in electrical current on the skin and in the brain, heart rate."

"If you found musical style A in a community," Lomax wrote, almost giddy with the sense of possibility, "you would know that a certain family of perhaps deeply hidden emotions was at play in the emotional and aesthetic life of the whole society…Folksong can become an index as to what is aesthetically wrong or right about a certain branch of the human family, or even with an individual." Or this, from a slightly later article published in an Italian journal: "By using the musical style as a diagnostic instrument, we can study the emotional and aesthetic story of the nations of the world…by using the analysis of the musical style as an instrument of prediction…we could reach *a technique of cultural planning*" (my italics).

In other words, the hypotheses he was evolving about the significance of aspects of musical style as applied to the supposed emotional lives of the communities that produced them could also be read backwards: the encouragement of certain musical techniques would tend to inculcate the desired emotional and aesthetic qualities in a given community, over time.

It is to Lomax's great credit that he did not let these kinds of theories determine what he recorded. While he was evolving this set of notions toward a comprehensive analysis of folk expression that could graph every constriction of the throat and toss of the head, label every last jump of a nerve, he was also able to maintain a boyish pleasure in, and even awe at, the moment of the expression. Then, "words, movement, ambition" would indeed be conquered by the Thing Itself, in all its uniqueness.

As all this was happening, the word from home was that the McCarthy era was fading into the past, and there was a serious revival of interest in folk music, especially among the young, and coming home began to seem like a good idea.

# 5.

Awakened in a new way to the world of the senses, and on fire with a vision of a unifying set of theories to explain it all, Alan Lomax came home in 1958 to a somewhat altered cultural and political landscape. When he had left, folklore as he practiced it had been the province of a very small group of people, none of whom were professional performers.

In the interim, interest had been stimulated by the reissuing on LP records of old recordings, most especially Harry Smith's *Anthology of American Folk Music* on Folkways Records, and Samuel Charters's book and companion LP *The Country Blues*. Recording equipment had gotten more portable, and younger men (they were mostly men) such as Mike Seeger, John Cohen, Ralph Rinzler, and others, some of whom not only collected the music but played and sang it on a professional level, began going out into the "field." Out of this activity came the rediscovery of early recording artists, many of whom had been heard on the *Anthology*, or *The Country Blues*—Mississippi John Hurt, Dock Boggs, Son House, Eck Robertson, and Bukka White, for example, as well as great musicians who had never been heard by a wide audience, such as Roscoe Holcomb and the autoharp virtuoso Kilby Snow. The new movement had sects of purists of various types, and the center of gravity had moved from Washington, D.C., to the Northeast—mainly New York City and Boston. In addition, communities of enthusiasts were sprouting up all over the country, in places as far flung as Minneapolis, San Francisco, and Iowa City.

Lomax, who had left the country as the more or less undisputed king of folk music collecting, returned as a kind of pope-in-exile, and it was a slightly bumpy reentry. All the younger generation of folk music aficionados had learned from and valued Lomax's recordings and contributions, through the Library of Congress and elsewhere, and Lomax-affiliated musicians such as Woody Guthrie and Leadbelly were saints of the movement. But there was something free and even anarchic about this new inquiry, and it bristled at any top-down theorizing or prescriptive discourse. Even Pete Seeger, who was every bit the man of the left that Lomax was, said of the late-1950s folk song revival that it was "out of the control of any person or party, right or left, purist or hybridist, romanticist or scientist."

Lomax, with his strong opinions and constant theorizing, ruffled many a feather. For example, he rapped what he called "citybillies" on the knuckles for performing material that spoke of emotions and experiences that they hadn't had. In an essay titled "The 'Folkniks' and the Songs They Sing," published in *Sing Out!* in 1959, he claimed that "in order to acquire a folk singing style, you have to experience the feelings that lie behind it, and learn to express them as the folksingers do." This could be a disastrous prescription; the best of the younger singers were in fact the ones who did not try and project themselves into the skin of a Parchman prisoner—how, after all, could they?—but approached the material as music.

If the new crop of folkies irritated Lomax, he was capable of irritating them right back. John Cohen, a member of the seminal folk revival group the New Lost City Ramblers, bristled at Lomax's emphasis on social reform, on using the music for an ulterior reason. "Lomax has presented himself," he wrote, also in *Sing Out!*, "as the 'holy ghost' sent from on high to deliver the gospel. He says, in effect, that he will lead us to the 'truth' if only we will follow him." His practice of copyrighting traditional material also offended many. John Greenway in a 1962 article for the journal *Western Folklore*, after claiming that Lomax "goes out of his way to annoy people who want desperately to like him," goes on to note, "Lomax has explained his need for protection against us pilfering folklorists, but I fear that many of our profession will go on using 'The Lass of Loch Royal' without paying Lomax any fee except a measure of acrimony."

That acrimony was not unanimous. In an early-1960s review in *Sing Out!* of Lomax's book *The Folk Songs of North America*, an anonymous reviewer derided "the pseudo-folklorists, self-made scholars, and the would-be Lomaxes who gather in little groups to make snide, sour-grapes jokes about the Messiah of American Folk Music..." and asserted that "I, for one, will stand behind Lomax's taste and judgment in guiding Americans into a knowledge of their all-but-forgotten heritage...no one is more able or qualified in such a capacity than Lomax." But it gives a hint of the jostling of egos in a newly open field at that time.

Lomax's response, in a sense, was to mount a kind of counteroffensive, a reconnaissance of the American South—its places and its people, in many of the locales that he had visited years before—to see for himself what had changed, and what had endured. He would bring along a new stereo tape recorder to document the singers and players—some of whom he had first met and recorded as much as two decades earlier—in clear and startlingly present sound quality. He would be accompanied by a young British folksinger named Shirley Collins, who was his assistant and lover, and who has provided us with her personal narrative of the trip's ups and downs. And he would bring his camera.

The first part of what came to be called the Southern Journey began in August 1959 and continued until October of that year. Starting in Salem, Virginia, Lomax and Collins wound their way through much of the southwestern part of the state, through Kentucky, down through Nashville to Alabama and into Mississippi, where they visited the prison farm at Parchman, as well as other spots mostly in the northern part of the state. They bounced back and forth between parts of Arkansas and Memphis, Tennessee before heading back across Mississippi, through Alabama again, en route to St. Simons Island off the Georgia coast.

They accomplished all this in under two months, and at a time when the interstate highway system was barely in its infancy and certainly hadn't penetrated the areas where they were headed. To this day, the roads in southeastern Virginia, as well as in the mountainous neighboring areas of Kentucky, Tennessee, and West Virginia, can be almost unbelievably tortuous when you leave the main highways. It is hard to imagine the difficulties of navigation fifty years ago as the duo made their way up and into "lonesome hollers, shady groves [and] heads of creeks," in Shirley Collins's words, to record people like Wade Ward, Hobart Smith, and Texas Gladden.

Adding to the logistical travail was the decision to camp out much of the time in order to save money. Collins vividly describes the conditions in her memoir *America Over the Water*. Quoting from a letter she sent home to England at the outset of their trip, she writes, "We arrived late in Salem and decided to camp out at the foot of the Blue Ridge Mountains. It took hours to get the tent up in the dark, Alan trying to hammer tent pegs into the very hard ground and waking up all the local dogs who barked furiously, me fussing about snakes and spiders. Alan got very cross, and when he finally crawled in onto his air mattress it collapsed!"

Still, the riches they were about to mine affected them both profoundly. The artists were for the most part commercially unrecorded, although several—among them Wade Ward, J. E. Mainer, and members of the Memphis Jug Band—had made a number of recordings some years earlier. Lomax's major finds, including Almeda Riddle and the great bluesman Fred McDowell, became irreplaceable figures; their contributions moved to the center of our understanding of traditional American music.

On the trip, Lomax recorded eighty hours of music and conversation on a stereo reel-to-reel tape recorder with new, expensive microphones that provided a sonic presence far beyond what he and his father had been able to achieve decades before. While the singers performed, or perhaps afterward, he took notes not only on the back of the tape boxes in the space provided—where he listed the names of the performers and the songs delivered, making notes on quality for use later on in selecting which performances would be issued on LP records—but also on the blank insides of the cardboard boxes, describing the singers' physical gestures, jotting down stray remarks or anecdotes.

An example, at random, from his October 6 visit with Neal Morris and Oscar Gilbert, in Timbo, Arkansas: *"He shakes his head like J.D.* [presumably referring to Morris's son, Jimmy Driftwood]—*smiles, raises his eyebrows—looks at you when he sings—closes his eyes on high notes. Watches his left hand on guitar … Oscar thinks & maintains Neal can sing better than Jimmie D. … Remember how O.G. sat & listened, mouthing the words as he listened to the playback …"* (page 99).

The boxes are encrusted, inside and out, with this kind of commentary, and it reflects his desire to somehow preserve the moment whole—not just the sound but the embodiment of the people and culture that produced it. And even as he was annotating, transcribing, and recording, he was preserving it all in yet another way, through the lens of his camera.

*Tape box from recording session at Mississippi State Penitentiary at Parchman, likely Camp B, Lambert, MS, September 19 or 20, 1959.*

Lomax did not keep a research notebook on the trip, instead writing scant notes on the tape boxes he used, alongside the list of songs recorded on each tape. He noted details about his subjects' lives, their style of playing, where and how they had learned to play their instruments, or the contents of the songs themselves. This particular tape box contains "Po' Laz'us," (Poor Lazarus) by inmate "James Carter and his group," which was famously used in the 2000 film *O Brother, Where Art Thou?* Sometimes Lomax's notes spilled over onto the back and inside of the tape box; here, on the inside cover of the box, he recorded notes about the prisoners he spoke to that day and what they talked about.

# 6.

Lomax's photos may be seen, in part, as a key to his deeper perceptions and sentiments, to a different and perhaps less conscious mythos. When one records people, one records them doing things that are recordable

*Baptism, near Mineola, TX, 1935.*

This photograph is part of a series of four images made during an outdoor submersion baptism ceremony conducted near Mineola, TX, 75 miles east of Dallas, during summer 1935. The images were taken from an embankment overlooking the rite and the more than 50 congregants gathered. The Lomaxes documented religious expression in various forms; by 1935 they had recorded sermons and singing in black, white, and Latino churches.

—singing, playing, telling stories. The results primarily reflect the subjects' repertoire, the subjects' abilities and limitations, the subjects' choices. But photographs are the record of the photographer's choice. Out of infinite possible moments, this one is chosen. What has the photographer chosen to see?

It is easy to recognize a family resemblance between these images and the work of the photographers affiliated with the Farm Security Administration of the mid- to late 1930s— Dorothea Lange, Arthur Rothstein, John Vachon, Jack Delano, and the rest. Lomax's ideology came

***Wilson "Stavin' Chain" Jones playing guitar and singing the ballad "Batson," Lafayette, LA, June 1934.***

In *Our Singing Country*, a collection of folk songs, Lomax and his father describe the experience of listening to Jones sing this 38-verse song about a white day laborer accused of murdering his employer and his family: "... no one who has ever heard him sing this wailing song with his guitar, at times beating a solemn dirge and then shrieking in hopeless despair can ever forget it. You've seen and felt a hanging. You notice, too, that the sympathies of the ballad singer rest wholly with the accused, not with his victims."

out of much the same New Deal bag. The FSA photographers had a mandate to focus on lives hitherto ignored or slighted, in the interests of awakening conscience and consciousness, making the case for social improvements and change. *Ecce homo*, the photos said; behold, and care for, your less advantaged brothers and sisters. They were designed, in the words of the FSA project director Roy Stryker, to "make a dent in the world."

One of the mysteries of the images in this book is that, while Lomax strongly shared that goal, his images seem to advance no agenda other than an appreciation of the subjects' sense of life. Even some of the finest FSA photographers—Rothstein, Lange, Walker Evans—often tended to "brand" their subjects, so that they became instruments of a statement about a larger vision—here is a poor Appalachian, here is his wretched bedroom, here is a bizarre or ironic juxtaposition of commercial imagery with urban decay, and so on.

In contrast, Lomax almost never argued for his subjects' abjectness or misery. He didn't have the pitiless, detached, consummate artist's eye of Walker Evans, nor did his pictures have the kind of *j'accuse* dimension of Rothstein's or Lange's, using images of dire straits to make a rhetorical point in which too often the human subjects are objectified. Nowhere is pathos depicted, or a political or even aesthetic point achieved, at the subject's expense. Lomax allowed his subjects a subjective life in his images; the very point was to deliver a sense of their subjective lives, rather than delivering them as objects, tools for a larger point. All of these photos say *Ecce homo* in a tone of generous acceptance. If the photos argue for any point, it is that people can make meaning and express beauty and fellowship even in the most dire circumstances. His photographs never attempt to usurp the dignity of their subjects.

Through Lomax's images, one enters a time continuum that is not dictated by the photographer. One telling sequence depicts a farm auction near Galax, Virginia, at which several musicians are playing on a porch. Lomax brings us in toward the music gradually, even cinematically, establishing the entire context first with a wide shot taking in the entire farm house, set on a hill, with a couple dozen men standing around, or sitting on the porch, talking. In the next shot we have moved much closer in and are being regarded with a degree of suspicion by several of the men sitting on the edge of the porch; behind them, we can see some musicians playing, one of them sitting on a porch swing. The next shot brings us right up onto the porch, where we are eye-to-eye with the three musicians—fiddler Uncle Charlie Higgins, guitarist Bob Carpenter, and, seated on the swing, Wade Ward, whom Alan had recorded over twenty years before on a previous collecting trip. But Lomax doesn't stop there; in two further shots he brings us, in effect, right into the circle of the musicians, with shots of all three in which their bodies and instruments are partly out of the frame, the camera is so close. The sequence is rounded out with a few more images—of men waiting for things to begin and of a group of women selling refreshments, and apparently having a better time than most of the men (pages 61–63).

He sometimes got so close in that he seemed to be trying to enter the musicians' skin. A photo of him recording Miles and Bob Pratcher on a porch in Como, Mississippi, shows how intimately he was involved in the recording process (page 91). Not only was there no control booth, as in a recording studio, but there was practically no physical separation between the musicians and Lomax. The same, more often than not, goes for the photographs. Later that same day in Como, Lomax took a photo of Ed Young playing fife and staring us right in the eye, with Lonnie Young Sr. in the foreground, crowding the camera (page 88). Similar images of the multi-instrumentalist and singer Hobart Smith (pages 60, 110, 113), the balladeer Texas Gladden (page 59), and others abound. Some of the most striking reveal the great and hitherto unrecorded bluesman Fred McDowell, shot from slightly below in a manner that lends them an almost monumental quality (page 95).

One place where Lomax and his companion Shirley Collins did not feel comfortable getting quite so close was near Blackey, Kentucky, where they tracked way back up a dirt path into the woods to document a Baptist prayer meeting. Collins, writing about the afternoon in *America Over the Water*, tells us, "The surroundings were pleasantly rural, but before long I started to feel nervous, fearful even. The people stared at us as we arrived and set up our recording equipment." After an hour or so one preacher began railing against their presence at the meeting, calling the recording equipment the work of the devil and predicting eternal damnation for the visitors. The photos of this meeting, and of Reverend I.D. Back preaching and gesturing, gives a vivid sense of the setting, the closeness of the bodies on benches and logs under the trees and on the rough platform (pages 72–73). Things did calm down eventually, but plainly the duo wasn't received with open arms in every instance. A sequence taken in a Hughes, Arkansas, juke joint late in the trip shows people gambling and drinking; their faces do not seem impressed with, welcoming of, or grateful for our attention (pages 96–97).

Certainly one of the most moving groups of photographs in this book presents prisoners on visiting day at the Mississippi State Penitentiary at Parchman. It is a companion sequence to another sequence, taken mostly in color, of prisoners at work in the sun, singing. As iconic as some of those outdoor images are, it is this other side of the story that pierces the heart—men in convict stripes in a common room, receiving children, wives, and girlfriends. Here, a convict on a bench looks up at the camera; standing in front of him is a young boy, probably his son, looking out at us from the shadow of his father's embrace (page 83). One man, seated next to a woman with his arm draped around her, smiles at the camera along with his companion (page 85). It could be an anniversary shot at a nightclub, except for those stripes. In perhaps the most moving image of all, one of the men is crouched down in front of a little girl who wears a white frock and sits on a bench holding a soda pop and listening intently to what the man is saying (page 84). The subtext of it all is that while these men are prisoners, and may have done bad and

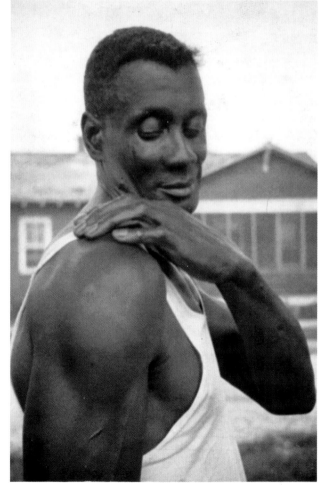

**John Bray, Amelia, LA, October 1934.**

Nicknamed Big Nig, Bray stood six feet, seven inches tall and worked sometimes as the singing leader of a gang that snaked cypress out of the Louisiana swamps. In his book *Adventures of a Ballad Hunter*, John A. Lomax wrote, "On our first visit we mistakenly tipped Big Nig in advance of his singing, only to find out later that he had become too drunk to sing. A year or so afterwards repeated visits put on record the singing and guitar picking of this remarkable man."

even hideous things, they are still, in a phrase to be found in more than one blues, "somebody's angel child" — or father or husband. And behind the images is also the clear echo of the emptiness that will be there when the families have gone.

As a photographer, Lomax was a resolute amateur, in the literal sense of loving his subjects and the process of taking photos, and probably proud of it. Instead of subsuming the human subject to a composition that would make a primarily aesthetic point, or using techniques to highlight or foreground a social point, Lomax showed his subjects expressing their own sense of life. Even the photos of the convicts at work do not seem to be primarily arguing against the injustice of their situation; the images argue, instead, if they argue for anything, for the humanity of the subjects. Even here, the images seem to say — even on this sagging porch or in this prison — people find a way to be human and to be together. With these images, Lomax drives that point home with, indeed, "glorious humanity."

Conditions were, of course, different in America in 1959 than they were in the Depression heyday of the FSA, it is true, but times were still tough, to say the least, in the areas where Lomax traveled. Within a couple years of Lomax's Southern Journey, national attention would be focused on Appalachia by the 1962 CBS television documentary *Christmas in Appalachia*, as well as books such as Michael Harrington's *The Other America* and Harry Caudill's *Night Comes to the Cumberlands*. And, of course, the Deep South locations in Mississippi and elsewhere were about to be hurled into the tumultuous waters of the civil rights movement.

So the troubled landscape of the Southern Journey was about to enter the consciousness of the entire nation, even as the consciousness of the rest of the nation was about to enter the world we see in the photos. It was a world rife with poverty and racism, problems that Lomax had spent most of his life thinking about and working against. Yet it was also a world that had developed precious and vulnerable cultural strategies for transmuting pain and travail into beauty through the sound of its musicians and singers, its tradition bearers. Almost as soon as Lomax left town, the bright light of media attention would change the cultural ecology of those places forever.

# 7.

To many of the people he documented, he must have appeared as a kind of conquistador, minus the swords and armor. One of the most telling images in this collection was taken by Shirley Collins, showing Lomax outside his car somewhere in southwestern Virginia, by a rickety bridge, cottages and hills in the background, face in the sun, taking the air (page 68). A happy man, arriving on a new continent full of possibility, his mission in at least one way the inverse of a conquistador's: he was there to make sure that the indigenous stayed indigenous.

In living rooms and on porches, in prisons and dance halls, he appeared bearing heavy recording equipment and an omnivorous curiosity. Most civilizations have to wait to be buried before being dug up; Lomax did the spade work in real time, before the body of expression had a chance to grow cold. Yet in the very act of documenting, of codifying, of *seeing*, inevitable distortions, however slight—shifts in emphasis, alterations of perspective—began to sprout in the delicate balance of a vanishing cultural world.

In 1963, John Davis, of the Georgia Sea Island Singers, one of the greatest musicians Alan recorded, made a telling remark to Lomax's sister Bess. Alan had recorded the Georgia singers on St. Simons Island toward the end of his Southern Journey, in October 1959, and the strength and grace of their group singing was almost overwhelming. Lomax brought them to festivals and nightclubs, and they became recognized and popular among folk music's mostly white audience. At the San Francisco club the Ash Grove during an engagement there, Davis told Bess Lomax Hawes, "Singing in front of these people might change what we do, because of what *they* do. We need someone to let us know if we're changing the way we do things."

The process that had begun in the 1920s, of searching out rural musicians to make commercial recordings, to build a market for those recordings, to brand them as "race records" or "Old-Time Tunes," had long since resulted in a degree of self-consciousness among performers who were pried out of their immediate context and repackaged for a national audience, often by selling a kind of preemptive nostalgia for a way of life that was only beginning to fade into the past.

In the twenty-odd years between Alan's first Southern collecting trips and his Southern Journey, that process had increased exponentially. By 1959, even the most rural singers and musicians had heard the refigurings of traditional music by the Carter Family and the countless others who had recorded in the ensuing decades. Yet Lomax tenaciously kept looking for music that hadn't been commodified, and which led back toward an at least partly mythical past before everything existed to make a profit. He had good luck, and great instincts, and he was able, in the waning light of the 1950s, before everything started to shake loose, to record some of the last of a breed, musicians and singers who had been influenced only minimally by the commercialization not just of the music but of the music's context.

And yet the people he recorded submitted to the process for a spectrum of reasons, including, for some, a sense that they were being "discovered." At the end of a church gospel performance that Lomax recorded in Tate County, Mississippi, the preacher announces to the congregation that there is a "talent scout" in the house! Fred McDowell plainly looked at Lomax in that way, too, and the recordings he made for him on that evening in Como, Mississippi, marked the beginning of an extraordinary career as a performer. There were others who, like McDowell, had the talent and desire and found careers in the 1960s folk revival—Hobart Smith, the Georgia Sea Island Singers. And then there were others who smelled something alien in the mix and expressed hostility, as had happened at the mountain revival outside Blackey, Kentucky.

At the confluence of these varied motives—documentary, commercial, expressive—sat Lomax, who was, himself, something of a battleground among these competing imperatives. Despite his own better angels, Lomax was not immune to the temptation to commodify what he saw. The early sixties saw the release of two separate series of long-playing records drawn from the Southern Journey material, one series released on Atlantic Records (which bankrolled the trip) and one on Prestige Records. Upon first release they were generally very well received by the folk audience, although they met some resistance in academic quarters.

Joseph Hickerson, writing in the journal *Ethnomusicology* in 1965, complains that these "field recordings" could not "be equated with the anthropologist's (and thence ethnomusicologist's) term, 'field work,' with its implications of hypothesis, method and technique.... Lomax seems mainly interested in obtaining stereophonic high fidelity recordings of the musicians, so that the lay listener and folk song enthusiast can hear the music as it 'really' is. His gauge, therefore, is the nature of the market for his recordings. These are certainly not the gauges of the scholar."

Such remarks must have hurt Lomax—doubly so because his own father had struggled against the same resistance. One can see here why he had something of a chip on his shoulder when it came to professional anthropologists, and why he felt he had something to prove. At the very same time that he was spreading the gospel of folk song and making it accessible to a national audience, he was also developing Cantometrics into a full-blown theory, his bid to establish a unifying theory of human expression, and to gain academic respect. A close examination of this set of theories is beyond the scope of this essay, but interested readers may read all about it in a number of essays included in the indispensable collection *Alan Lomax: Selected Writings, 1934–1997*, edited by historian Ronald D. Cohen.

The paradoxes in Lomax's own personality and intentions became, in a sense, the paradoxes in his ethnographic philosophy. The tensions between the impulse toward personal immediacy and analytical codification, and between the academic stance and the desire to popularize, marked his life and work from the beginning. His career was a tug-of-war between a profound respect for the indigenous expressions of culture and a relentless desire both to make those expressions assimilable to as broad an audience as possible and to evolve some system, some narrative, that could lend them all a common mythos.

It is not going too far to say that these efforts sometimes contained a dimension that could with justice be called paternalistic. In the early 1930s, in a proposal for a grant from the Carnegie Foundation, Lomax wrote that "The Negro in the South is the target for such complex influences that it is hard to find genuine folk singing," and he partly blamed the educational system for "broadening his concepts and thus making him ashamed or self-conscious of his own art." He followed this line through his life. In a mid-1970s article entitled "Appeal for Cultural Equity," he wrote, "When we 'educate' a non-European, especially when we teach him Western music or art or dance, as if no other system existed or had such value, we are brainwashing him. The standard Western European system of music education, taken to other cultural settings, is a form of aesthetic imperialism that is as destructive of native musical autonomy as the takeover of political and economic power is destructive of native initiative."

From one angle, this can be read as the template for multicultural respect. From another, it could appear to be a desire to keep people, in a figurative as well as a literal sense, in their place. Why, after all, shouldn't an African American from Mississippi become a classical pianist? Or a Japanese violinist become one of the great classical players in the world? Lomax was able to make the decision to "forget Beethoven and all that," since the decision was his to make. But you can't forget what you never knew in the first place. In any case, it is an unresolved irony in the thought and career of a man who in almost every way stood for freedom and human dignity.

In April of 1960 the Colonial Williamsburg Foundation hired Alan Lomax as music supervisor for *Music of Williamsburg*. The film was produced to give tourists a sense of daily life in Colonial-era Virginia and, according to a 1962 press release from the foundation, "to portray the important contributions of the Negro race to the nation's heritage." Lomax researched the period and its music, and brought the Spiritual Singers of Coastal Georgia (later the Georgia Sea Island Singers) together with Bahamian drummer Nat Rahmings, Mississippi Hill Country fife blower Ed Young, and Appalachian multi-instrumentalist Hobart Smith. Among these images we come upon one revealing moment, a glimpse of black Mississippian Ed Young playing fife with the white Virginian Hobart Smith, and the image seems so natural to us today that it may take a minute to realize that it is the only photograph in this entire portfolio of a black and a white musician playing together.

If in the "field" photos taken the previous year we can see Lomax's empathy and humility at its highest level, these qualities are more difficult to locate in the Williamsburg series, in which the subjects have been dressed up in "period" style, posed, and manipulated to serve the film's narrative purposes. The resulting photos, many of them staged shots, unsurprisingly lack some of the sense of life, and the vivid moment, to be found in the field photos. That being said, there are extraordinary faces to be found, here—especially the regal Bessie Jones, of the Georgia Sea Island Singers.

For the rest of his life, after this extraordinary and fortuitous exploration into a world that was about to disappear forever, Alan Lomax kept doing what he had always done, in the arenas of politics, culture, and folklore. He became a member of the board of the enormously important and influential Newport Folk Festival, continued his traveling and collecting activities with time in the Caribbean, continued his work with Cantometrics and expanded the idea to cover dance, a field he termed Choreometrics, produced the fine *American Patchwork* series

***Inmates chopping wood, State (Reid) Farm, Boykin, SC, December 1934.***

John A. Lomax made four disc recordings, about 40 minutes in total length, during his December 1934 stop in Boykin, SC. He recorded a gospel quartet and, as suggested by this photograph, a group of prisoners singing work songs. The elder Lomax saw the prisons as convenient repositories for all manner of folk songs. In his contribution to the 1935 *Report of the Librarian of Congress*, he wrote, "[T]hrough the black men and women convicts brought together in a State penitentiary one can get a fair cross section of the folk songs current in any district of the South.... To go to a penitentiary for this type of material is simply a short cut to covering any section in the shortest period of time and at the least expense."

of music documentaries, received the National Medal of the Arts from President Reagan, and wrote the very powerful book *The Land Where the Blues Began*. John Szwed's recent biography, *Alan Lomax: The Man Who Recorded the World*, is an excellent overview of this brilliant, deeply contradictory, and finally heroic life.

When, in 1967, Lomax published the song collection *Hard-Hitting Songs for Hard-Hit People* (compiled and edited with Pete Seeger and Woody Guthrie in the 1940s), the book was illustrated with photographs largely chosen from the FSA catalogue, as appropriate running testimony to the messages contained in the songs. The combination of the photos and the no-holds-barred songs lent the book an inescapable aura of agitprop. And yet when Lomax himself was behind the camera, he put the emphasis in a different place—not ignoring the hard conditions, but singing the beauty of the people who sang despite those conditions. Behind all the outsized achievements, the theorizing, the advocacy, the restless traveling, there remained alive the very young man whose life was changed utterly by the experience—beyond theory and analysis—of hearing the live nerve of a nation's music, its very soul, transmitted, in the vivid present, by people considered expendable by most of the population. That transfiguring moment became the animating spirit in all the work he was to do. It lives in all the recordings he made. And Lomax's own experience, the deepest part, perhaps, of his own soul, lives in these very human, very open, and immeasurably valuable images from the lost world he had found.

LIST OF POSSESIONS AND EQUIPMENT CARRIED BY CAR ON TRIP THROUHH

SOUTHERN STATEES...

1) One Altec lipstick mike....     $ 300.00  *225.00*
2) RCA D77 Mikes...    each $200   $ 600.00  *398.00*
3) One Power amplifier wi th
     stereo mizing box...            100.00
4) One six channel , passive mizer   100.00  *200.00*
7) One pr. stero earphones            25.00  *50.00*
8) Three mike stands                 150.00  *45.00*
9) Cables (5)                         30.00
10) One 12 volt battery               12.00  *32.00*
11) One battery charger               10.00
12) One vibrator convertor..          30.00  *45.00*
13)  2 mike mountings                 10.00

14) 50 12 in reels of tape           110.00

15) One rortary convertor            100.00
16) One Martin guitar                150.00
17) One Clifford Essex banjo          75.00
18) One Olivetti Studio typewriter   110.00
19) One suitcase containing
     two suits, six shirts, towels , etc.. ...
                                     150.00
20) One box books                     50.00
21) One suitcase, containing
     personal belongings             175.00

22) One hold-all valise...           100.00
     with contents...
23) One carrying case  containing
     Contax camera                   100.00
     Minetape machine with
       accessories                   ~~150.00~~
                                     350.00
     One aires camera                 75.00

24) Two tennis rackets                30.00
25 ) One tent                         14.00
26) Two matteress and sleeping bags   50.00
27) One 601-2 Ampex stero recorder
                                    1000.00
                                    ----------
                                    *3784.00*

# The Southern Journey

LEFT PAGE:

THIS typed packing list shows the equipment that Lomax brought on the Southern Journey and the value of each item. Besides the recording and camera equipment, he managed to squeeze in two tennis rackets, but he likely did not encounter many tennis courts during the course of the trip.

ALAN LOMAX first recorded Texas Gladden in 1941. Gladden sang ballads and songs rooted in the British Isles, as well as regional songs. Gladden knew more than 300 songs by memory, having learned them from her family, from factory coworkers, and from radio and records. She told Alan, "I have a perfect mental picture of every song I sing." At the start of the Southern Journey, Alan went to Gladden's house in Salem, Virginia, then to see her brother Hobart Smith, in Bluefield, Virginia.

*Texas Gladden and unidentified man,*
*likely her husband, Jim, Salem, VA, August 24, 1959.*

ALAN initially recorded Hobart Smith in 1942 and revisited him on the Southern Journey. Like his sister Texas Gladden, Hobart Smith grew up with music. He played fiddle, guitar, piano, and banjo. On this last instrument he was so skilled that musician Bill Monroe, the Father of Bluegrass, called him "the best old-time banjo picker I ever heard." As a young man, Smith played in minstrel shows and had his own string ensemble, the Hobart Smith Band. He performed at land auctions, society events, dances, baptisms, and church. "Old-timey music," he said in an interview, "I love it better than anything." Nonetheless, music was never more than a side project for Smith, and he worked variously as a farmer, wagon driver, house painter, and butcher. He died in 1965.

RIGHT PAGE:

IN Galax, Virginia, Alan Lomax reconnected with a longtime associate, Wade Ward. "Uncle Wade," as he was known, played fiddle and clawhammer banjo. John A. Lomax and Alan Lomax recorded him multiple times—John as early as 1937, when Ward was a member of the Bogtrotters Band, and Alan for the last time in 1959. During the Southern Journey Alan captured Ward performing with fiddler Charlie Higgins and guitarist Bob Carpenter at a farm auction, seen here.

*Top: Farm auction near Galax, VA, August 29, 1959.*
*Bottom: Uncle Charlie Higgins (with fiddle), Bob Carpenter (with guitar), Wade Ward (with banjo), and unidentified men, farm auction near Galax, VA, August 29, 1959.*

*Uncle Charlie Higgins (with fiddle), Bob Carpenter (with guitar), and Wade Ward (with banjo), farm auction near Galax, VA, August 29, 1959.*

*Glen Stoneman with fiddle (top), and unidentified fiddler (bottom),*
*Hillsville, VA, August 29, 1959.*

*Shirley Collins in car near Galax, VA, August 29, 1959.*

SHIRLEY COLLINS was Lomax's assistant and constant companion on the 1959 leg of the Southern Journey. In 1993 Alan sent her a copy of his book *The Land Where the Blues Began* in which he had inscribed "With much love and great admiration to one of the sweetest singers and ladies who ever walked and graced the green ways of this earth." Receiving the book inspired Shirley to write her memoir of the 1959 trip, *America Over the Water*.

*Wade Ward listening to playback with Alan Lomax at the Ward home,*
*Galax, VA, August 31, 1959.*

*Alan Lomax standing by his car (top), and a homestead (bottom), unidentified location in southwest VA, August 29 to 31, 1959.*

*Ballad singer Horton Barker, Chilhowie, VA, September 3, 1959.*

HORTON BARKER was a much-documented blind ballad singer from southwest Virginia who first came to prominence at the 1930s White Top Folk Festival in Virginia. Barker's version of "The Farmer's Curst Wife," issued on the Library's *Anglo-American Ballads* (1942), was learned and disseminated widely by younger performers. Barker wryly tells the story of a farmer interrupted one day when the devil arrives to claim a member of his family. The farmer suggests his wife, but she proceeds to abuse the devil and his minions so excessively that they bring her back to the old man. Sings Barker, "There's one advantage women have over men; they can go to Hell and come back again. Sing heigh, diddle-eye, diddle-eye fie! Diddle-eye, diddle-eye, day!"

BORN in Tennessee in 1919, Spencer Moore's love of old-time music began early and, at the age of 14, he attended the famous White Top Folk Festival. In the late 1930s, playing with his brother Joe as the Moore Brothers, Moore played a tent show with the Carter Family. At the time Lomax visited, Moore was a tobacco farmer known locally for playing on the *Farm & Fun Time Radio Show* out of Bristol. In 2003 Moore performed at the Alan Lomax Tribute concert in New York City alongside celebrated musicians such as Honeyboy Edwards, Arlo Guthrie, and Pete Seeger, among others.

THE Southern Journey was Shirley Collins's first visit to America. As she and Alan toured the South in his big Buick, she marveled at the region's landscapes. From Virginia she wrote to her parents in England that "All the folks we record live way back in the Blue Ridge Mountains, in lonesome hollers, shady groves, heads of creeks." The Cumberland Gap on the Tennessee-Kentucky border was "such a beautiful and fertile valley that I wondered why the Kentuckians had chosen to stay in the tangled wilderness of the mountains." The Mississippi Delta, "flat and wide as far as the eye can see," made Collins feel very far from home. And east of the Delta, Mississippi's Hill Country, she noted that "It was very dry here, the soil so eroded that there were great cracks in the earth as wide as the car's wheel."

THESE photos were taken at an outdoor service of the Mount Olivet Old Regular Baptist Church, staged in the woods outside of Blackey, Kentucky. The service was led by the Reverend I.D. Back. Each song was lined out lyric by lyric, sung first by a preacher and then by the congregants. Their singing voices, Collins wrote, were "harsh, strangled and fervent…a heart-stopping sound of people in torment." She became frightened when one preacher delivered a fiery sermon in which he condemned her haircut and Lomax's recording equipment. Another preacher was more accepting of the strangers and said, "Why, this young man and his little contraptions might be the means of someone knowing that the songs of Zion are still being sung."

THE Lomaxes first made recordings in Kentucky in 1933, and in 1937 Alan returned to eastern Kentucky with his wife Elizabeth, recording 228 discs full of ballads, fiddle tunes, white gospel, children's songs, and union songs. Two recordings from the 1937 trip in particular have influenced American popular culture:

William Stepp's version of the fiddle tune "Bonaparte's Retreat," later replicated as Aaron Copland's "Hoedown" from the ballet *Rodeo*; and Georgia Turner's "Rising Sun Blues," which became the rock standard "House of the Rising Sun."

Like Alan's earlier Kentucky trips, the 1959 field trip, again limited to eastern Kentucky,

focused primarily on religious expression. Alan made seven tapes likely on one day, September 6, 1959, in two locations. First stop was this outdoor sermon in Blackey—the images of I.D. Back's charismatic preaching provide striking documentation—then on to an indoor service in Mayking, Kentucky.

*Reverend I.D. Back preaching to the congregation of Mount Olivet Old Regular Baptist Church.*

*Ada Combs playing banjo for children on her porch (top) and the outside of her home (bottom), Whitesburg, KY, c. September 7, 1959.*

ADA COMBS was an 86-year-old banjo player who lived alone in a mountain shack a few miles from the nearest road in Whitesburg, Kentucky. She greeted Lomax and Collins wearing her best—and only—dress and carrying an "old wooden banjo...bedecked with purple ribbons" in her "brilliantly varnished fingers." Although her hands were shaking too badly to play more than a few songs, she entertained her visitors with stories about topics ranging from snake handlers to murder, square dances, and rearing children.

*Used furniture store, Whitesburg, KY, c. September 7, 1959.*

*DeFord Bailey, Nashville, TN, likely September 8–11, 1959.*

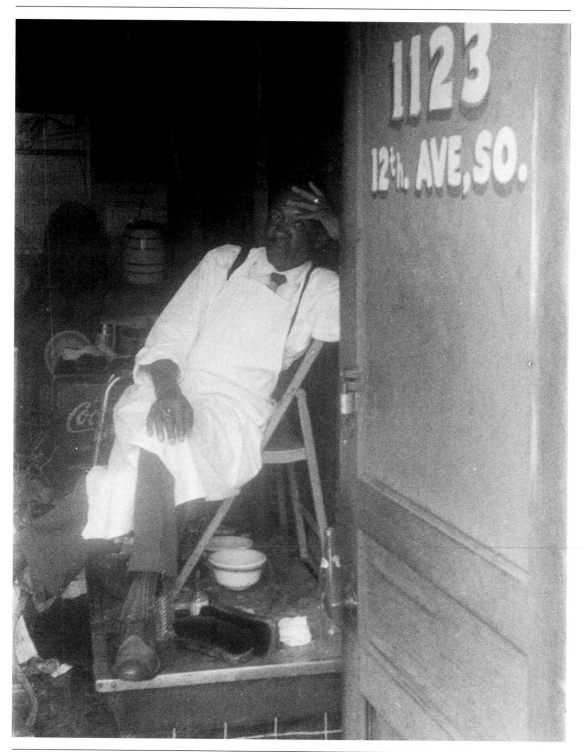

*DeFord Bailey, Nashville, TN, likely September 8–11, 1959.*

THE grandson of slaves, DeFord Bailey grew up in a family where "Everyone could play at least one instrument." Bailey learned to play the harmonica, or mouth harp, at the age of three when he was confined to bed for a year with infantile paralysis (polio). Bailey performed regularly on WSM's radio show the *Grand Ole Opry*. In 1941, after fifteen seasons, he was fired due to a licensing dispute, an occurrence that Opry historian Charles Wolfe called "one of the great tragedies of American music." For the rest of his life, Bailey made a living by shining shoes and renting out rooms in his house. Although he no longer played professionally, he continued to play for his friends and customers, including at the storefront pictured here, at 1123 12th Avenue in Nashville.

*Inmates chopping wood, Mississippi State Penitentiary, likely Camp B, Lambert, MS, September 19 or 20, 1959.*

BEGINNING in 1933, Alan Lomax and his father, John A. Lomax, made several field trips to the Mississippi State Penitentiary at Parchman. In 1933 they brought the state-of-the-art instantaneous disc recorder to Parchman hoping to capture the harmonic complexity and dynamic range of the communal work songs, but the results were predictably unsatisfactory. In 1947 Alan employed newly available magnetic open reel tape. Not only was the fidelity improved, but he could record long stories and interviews. By 1959 he added stereo microphones and brought to bear a quarter century of fieldwork experience.

Over the course of five days, Lomax visited Parchman Camps 7 and 11, and Camp B in Lambert, about 25 miles northeast of Parchman, making nine 7-inch open reel recordings, 35 color images, and 88 black-and-white images. Alan wrote in *The Land Where the Blues Began*: "The faces of the prisoners, so shadowy and fawning in repose, so fiery and powerful in song, their touching and powerful melodies, their graceful, golden voices, all conspired to win our allegiance."

*Inmates chopping wood, Mississippi State Penitentiary, likely Camp B,*
*Lambert, MS, September 19 or 20, 1959.*

COMMUNAL work songs are an African tradition, but Alan Lomax reported that he and his father "discovered that every state pen had developed distinctive work-song styles…This vein of African American creativity flourished in the state pens because there it was essential to the spiritual as well as the physical survival of the black prisoners." In prison, work songs were sung during tree cutting, cane cutting, cotton picking, and hoeing in order to relieve tension, to keep time, and to prevent prison guards from singling out any one worker as slower than the others.

THE Mississippi State Penitentiary, the oldest prison in Mississippi, was established in 1901 when the state ceased its convict leasing system. Nicknamed Parchman after its first warden, Jim Parchman, the prison was run like a large plantation. Inmates worked ten-hour days, six days a week, to produce livestock and raise crops, especially cotton. Lomax wrote, "The land produced the same crop and blacks had the same work to do on both sides of the wire fence…But every Delta black knew how easily he could find himself on the wrong side of that fence." At the time Lomax visited, Parchman had about 2,000 inmates living in segregated prison camps. Camp B in Lambert, where many of these pictures were taken, was one of the largest African American camps.

*Prison official and inmate on porch, Mississippi State Penitentiary, likely Camp B, Lambert, MS, September 19 or 20, 1959.*

PARCHMAN was an unforgiving place and prison officials could be cruel. Lomax wrote that, "Hired on because of their high qualifications as 'nigger drivers,' the Southern penologists joyously and self-righteously humiliated, bullied, beat, often tortured, and sometimes murdered their charges." The "trusty system"—in which trustworthy inmates were given rifles and charged with disciplining fellow inmates —encouraged abuse, and whippings with "Black Betty," a thick leather strap, were common. Alan harshly criticized Southern prison farms, calling them "a chain of hellholes strung across the land like so many fiery crosses to remind Southern blacks that chains and armed guards and death awaited them if they rebelled."

*Inmate with visiting children in dining hall, Mississippi State Penitentiary,*
*likely Camp B, Lambert, MS, September 19 or 20, 1959.*

*Inmate with visiting children in dining hall, Mississippi State Penitentiary,*
*likely Camp B, Lambert, MS, September 19 or 20, 1959.*

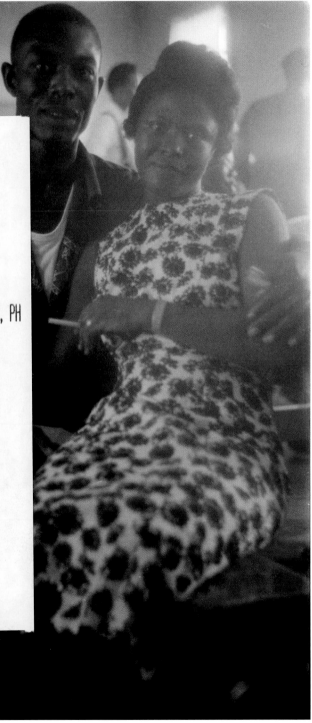

# Godkin, Dax

User name: Godkin, Dax

Item ID: 0000621545664

Title: SOUTHERN JOURNEY OF ALAN LOMAX: WORDS, PH

OTOGRAPH

Current time: 05/05/2015,8:27

*Inmate and visiting woman dancing in dining hall, Mississippi State Penitentiary,
likely Camp B, Lambert, MS, September 19 or 20, 1959.*

*Inmate and visitor, Mississippi State Penitentiary, likely Camp B, Lambert, MS, September 19 or 20, 1959.*

AT Parchman, family visits were allowed for two hours each Sunday. At that time, Mississippi was the only state to allow conjugal visits, a practice that began unofficially at Parchman around 1918. Thought to encourage good behavior, preserve marriages and families, and reduce homosexuality, conjugal visits took place in what prisoners called the "red houses," small, long buildings that had between five and ten rooms. Although only married couples were allowed conjugal visits, Lomax wrote that "guards and trusties were kept happy with various kinds of payoffs" and some "wives" were actually prostitutes.

BROTHERS Ed and Lonnie Young, along with Lonnie's son, Lonnie Jr., entertained at country picnics around Como, Mississippi. The father and son were drummers. Ed Young played the fife—or, as he called it, the "fice."

As the Young brothers played at Ed Young's home, their relatives emerged to dance to the music. Lomax wrote, "Watching the Young brothers' line of fife and drums sashay across the yard, enclosed by their dancing family, I saw in my mind's eye the jazz parades of New Orleans, where the band is a pulsing artery in the belly of a huge dancing throng. I remembered the Mardi Gras parades in Trinidad and Rio and the wild *rara* parades of Haiti and the films I'd seen of African processionals, and I could see that this family party in northern Mississippi belonged to that African tradition."

*Lonnie Young Sr. (with bass drum) at the home of Ed Young, Como, MS, September 21, 1959.*

"ONCE you looked closely, you saw that the mainspring of the action was Lonnie and his bass drum," Lomax wrote in *The Land Where the Blues Began.* "Movements flowed from Lonnie's midsection throughout his body. He played the lead in the band's polyrhythm, his padded sticks making a low, murmurous, but heated comment on the squeals of Ed Young's fife, as G. D. Young, the little brother of the bunch, riffled the snare drum."

*Miles Pratcher (with guitar), Bob Pratcher (with fiddle) and Shirley Collins*
*on Miles Pratcher's porch, Como, MS, September 22 or 23, 1959.*

THE "elderly Pratcher brothers," Collins wrote, played with the "same quality that, for me, defined the black music of that part of Northern Mississippi, a buoyant drive, no matter what the age of the musician."

*Alan Lomax (with recorder), on Miles Pratcher's porch,*
*Como, MS, September 22 or 23, 1959.*

*Lucius Smith (with banjo) on Sid Hemphill's porch,*
*Senatobia, MS, September 22 or 23, 1959.*

ALAN first recorded Sid Hemphill and the archaic music traditions—panpipes and fife and drum bands, among other genres—of the Mississippi Hill Country during his 1942 field trip to the Delta, part of a socioeconomic study of that region undertaken by the Library of Congress and a team from Fisk University. He returned in September 1959 with a decade of intensive documentary experience in Europe and a new stereo tape recorder. Lomax later recalled that as he watched Sid and his friend Lucius Smith play, "it dawned on me that on that dust-laden summer afternoon…I had stumbled onto an outcropping of African music in North America."

RIGHT PAGE:

LOMAX called Sid Hemphill "the boar-hog musician of the hills" and "the blind musical maestro of Panola County." The 91-year-old Hemphill, who could play nine different instruments, including the quills, or panpipes, shown here, delivered a memorable performance with his friend Lucius Smith on banjo. Shirley Collins wrote that "they played with a zest and energy that belied their age. It was wonderfully attractive, this combination of African sounds and Southern dance tunes."

This photograph is one in a series of images of these girls at play and illustrates Lomax's ongoing interest in children's songs and games, which began during his earliest travels to the Caribbean.

*Fred McDowell (top) and Rosalie Hill (bottom) on Fred McDowell's porch, Como, MS, September 24, 1959.*

"I SHALL never forget," wrote Shirley Collins, "the first sight I had of Fred in his dungarees, carrying his guitar and walking out of the woods toward us in a Mississippi night." Of all the musicians recorded on the Journey, Fred McDowell became the most famous. Lomax recorded him over four nights in 1959 because during the day McDowell was busy picking cotton. A sharecropper who sang and played slide guitar in juke joints and at dances, he embodied a legacy of black work songs and field hollers. When he performed his "61 Highway Blues" for Lomax, the folklorist wrote a single word beside the entry in his field log: "Perfect."

*Couple at Charlie Houlin's juke joint,*
*Hughes, AR, October 1, 1959.*

*Gambler (left) and Forrest City Joe B. Pugh (right) at Charlie Houlin's juke joint, Hughes, AR, October 1, 1959.*

BLUES MUSICIANS Memphis Slim, Big Bill Broonzy, and Sonny Boy Williamson recommended that Lomax seek out Charlie Houlin, a white man in Hughes, Arkansas, whom they all considered a friend. (Houlin was rumored to have shot and killed a white sheriff in order to protect a black friend.)

These photos were taken at his juke joint, Houlin's Place. Houlin directed Lomax to the musician Forrest City Joe B. Pugh, a nimble harmonica and piano player and the front man of a band called Forrest City Joe and His Three Aces. To record the band, Lomax set up his stereo equipment on the bar of a crowded honky-tonk. "Between takes," he wrote later, "the place was a bedlam, but the emotional atmosphere was mellow and marvelous…The crowd danced during all the playbacks."

NEAL MORRIS was the father of folksinger-songwriter Jimmy Driftwood. Driftwood wanted Lomax and Collins to meet his father, whom he said had given him a musical education. With a voice that Collins described as "light, melodious, and full of character," Morris played more than a dozen songs, including "Turkey in the Straw," "Turnip Greens," "The Lass of Loch Royale," and "The Banks of the Arkansas." In his notes, Lomax wrote "smiles, raises his eyebrows—looks at you when he sings—closes his eyes on high notes…"

DESPITE a reputation for a fiery temper, 75-year-old Oscar Gilbert "was a fine and gentle singer," according to Collins. He sang the outlaw ballad "Cole Younger" and a religious song, "Go Preaching Through the Wilderness," and played the fiddle for his visitors. His wife, Ollie, also knew many songs, including several ballads rooted in the British Isles.

*Almeda Riddle with Shirley Collins (foreground) at Riddle's home, Greers Ferry, AR, c. October 6 or 7, 1959.*

ALMEDA Riddle, one of America's most important ballad singers, was first recorded in 1952, by folklorist John Quincy Wolf. Riddle's father had taught in shape-note singing schools, which is how she first heard many of the hundreds of songs she knew. Without instrumental accompaniment she could sing ballads, hymns, and children's songs. In 1926 a tornado killed her husband and one of her sons and destroyed her home, along with the household trunk in which Riddle kept her handwritten collection of ballads. Fortunately, she had memorized most of them. About her repertoire she said, "These things that have come down orally over the centuries had to be the cream of the crop, or they'd have died out a long time ago."

IN October Lomax briefly returned to Parchman. On this visit he met John Dudley at Parchman Farm Dairy Camp, where Dudley was serving the last months of a prison sentence. Dudley sang country blues with slide guitar. Dudley told Lomax that he did most of his playing in the mid- and late twenties, at "old country balls" in Tunica County, Mississippi, where he was from. When Lomax asked Dudley how he knew a certain song, Dudley responded, "Just picked it up myself…just learned it."

*Vera Ward Hall at her home, Livingston, AL, October 10, 1959.*

THOUGH she worked for most of her life as a domestic servant, Vera Ward Hall is remembered today for her voice. John A. Lomax and Ruby Terrill Lomax recorded her in 1937. On the Southern Journey, Alan reconnected with her at her home in Livingston, Alabama. He wrote later: "The sound comes from deep within her...from a source of gold and light." Hall knew spirituals, children's songs, and blues.

In 2000, half a lifetime after her death in 1964, pop artist Moby released the single "Natural Blues." The song returned Hall to the public consciousness by sampling her "Trouble So Hard," recorded by Lomax in October 1959.

B Y the second week of October 1959, Alan and Shirley Collins made it to the Georgia coast, to the Sea Islands, whose singers Alan had first recorded a quarter century earlier. Lomax believed that Sea Island music linked America to West Africa and that this body of songs is today "probably unmatched for singability and worldwide popularity." At this point the 1959 leg of the Southern Journey was over and the pair drove north to New York, with Collins continuing home to England. The documentary tally after driving through eight states over a challenging seven-week span, August 24 through October 12, 1959: 85 tapes, 538 photographs. Alan would return to Tidewater, Virginia, and to the Georgia Sea Islands in April and May 1960, assisted by his daughter Anna Lomax, to record an additional 17 tapes and 266 photographs.

ALAN spent much of the winter and spring of 1960 preparing material for the film *The Music of Williamsburg*, an educational film promoting Colonial Williamsburg. Alan was tasked with finding talent and material that would represent eighteenth century traditional music. For this, he drew upon acquaintances from the Southern Journey: Hobart Smith, the banjo player from Virginia, Ed Young, the fifer from Mississippi, and the Georgia Sea Island Singers. The latter portrayed slaves in the film, contributing their archaic dance styles and song repertoire. The Williamsburg project, then, provided a fitting coda to the Southern Journey, throughout which Lomax and Collins had sought the music and performers of the past.

*Bessie Jones (seated on right) and cast on the set of the* Music of Williamsburg *film, Williamsburg, VA, April 25–27, 1960.*

BESSIE JONES was the only mainlander, or non-islander, admitted into the ranks of the Georgia Sea Island Singers. Her four grandparents were born into slavery, and they taught her as a child about slave life, including music. She moved to St. Simons Island after marrying a native, and she brought to the Singers a host of gospel songs, party games, ring shouts, and hollers.

THE leader of the Georgia Sea Island Singers, John Davis, decided what songs they sang and who sang each part. Lomax first met Davis in the 1930s. Between that time and the Southern Journey, Davis traveled the world as a seaman. Resettled on St. Simons Island by 1960, he was farming and fishing when Lomax invited the Singers to the film shoot in Williamsburg, Virginia.

*Bessie Jones (top) and Hobart Smith (bottom), Williamsburg, VA, April 25–27, 1960.*

*John Davis (right), Mable Hillery, Ed Young (with soda bottle),*
*and members of the Georgia Sea Island Singers, Williamsburg, VA, April 25–27, 1960.*

*Ed Young (with fife) and Hobart Smith (with banjo),*
*Williamsburg, VA, April 25–27, 1960.*

*On the set of the* Music of Williamsburg *film,*
*Williamsburg, VA, April 25–27, 1960.*

LOMAX wrote that the way Ed Young crouched and danced while playing the fife reminded him of Pan, the Greek god of rustic music. In *The Land Where the Blues Began*, he described Young thus: "He always danced as he played, his feet sliding along flat to the ground to support his weaving pelvis, enticing someone in the crowd to cut it with him, turning this way and that, always with dragging feet and bent knees, and always leaning toward the earth."

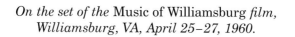

*Members of the Church of God and Saints of Christ a cappella choir,*
*Belleville, VA, April 30, 1960.*

THE Church of God and Saints of Christ is a black Jewish-Christian church. It was established in Kansas in 1896 and is headquartered in Suffolk, Virginia. Lomax made 2 tape recordings and 17 photographs of the church's choir in nearby Belleville. The National Chorus of the Church of God and Saints of Christ, which passes down its spirituals orally, was a featured performer at the symposium *The Lomax Legacy: Folklore in a Globalizing Century,* held at the Library of Congress in January 2006. The symposium celebrated the acquisition by the American Folklife Center, Library of Congress, of the Alan Lomax Collection.

*Bishop Twine outside of the Union Holiness Church,*
*Portsmouth, VA, May 1, 1960.*

AT the time Lomax took these pictures, Bishop Charles Atlas Twine was 100 years old and had been preaching at the Union Holiness Church for 50 years. Twine founded the Pentecostal church in 1910 with about twenty members who met at the local Firemen's Hall and was its pastor until his death in 1963, at age 103. Today the church is known as Twine Memorial Holy Temple.

# Selected Sources

Clar, Mimi. "The Blues Jump a Rabbit." *Western Folklore* 21, no. 3 (July 1962): 223–28.

Cohen, Ronald D. "The Folk Revival (1960s)." *Alan Lomax: Selected Writings, 1934–1997.* New York: Routledge, 1997 (187–94).

Collins, Shirley. *America Over the Water: A Musical Journey with Alan Lomax.* London: S. A. F. Publishing Limited, 2004.

"Folk Albums Taped in Dixie Fields by Prestige." *Chicago Daily Defender (Daily Edition)* (October 25, 1962): 21.

"Folk Music of Africa Put on Records Here." *Chicago Defender (National Edition)* (December 10, 1960): 18.

Greenway, John. "Some Superlatives, Old and New." *Western Folklore* 20, no. 2 (April 1961): 147–52.

Greenway, John. "For the Folklorists' Basic Library." *Western Folklore* 21, no. 4 (October 1962): 294–98.

Hansen, Barry, Paul Nelson, and Jon Pankake. "Alan Lomax." *Little Sandy Review* 10 (September 1961?): 3–26.

Hickerson, Joseph C. "Alan Lomax's 'Southern Journey': A Review-Essay." *Ethnomusicology* 9, no. 3 (September 1965): 313–22.

Lomax, Alan. *The Land Where the Blues Began.* New York: The New Press, 1993.

Oakes, Jason. "Harp of a Thousand Strings, All Day Singing from the Sacred Harp." *Yearbook for Traditional Music* 31 (1999): 187–88.

Oja, Carol J. "Filming the Music of Williamsburg with Alan Lomax." Institute for Studies in American Music newsletter, Fall 2003 (Brooklyn College of CUNY).

Pen, Ron. "Family Values: The Lomax Family and American Folksong." *College Music Symposium* 38 (1998): 156–63.

Shelton, Robert. "Country Blues: Growing Field for Research." *New York Times* (December 11, 1960): X15.

Shelton, Robert. "Folksong Realities Are Out in the Field." *New York Times* (October 21, 1962): 140.

Szwed, John. *Alan Lomax: The Man Who Recorded the World.* New York: Viking, 2010.

Tyrell, William G. "Recordings Not to Be Missed: Sounds of the South." *Sing Out!* 11, no. 1 (February–March 1961): 81–82.

Wilgus, D. K. "Record Reviews." *Journal of American Folklore* 76, no. 301 (July–September 1963): 272–74.

Yates, Michael. "Reviews, Sound Recordings: The Alan Lomax Collection." *Folk Music Journal* 7, no. 4 (1998): 525–34.

# Music-CD Track List

Additional music that Lomax recorded on his Southern Journey can be streamed online at research.culturalequity.org/audio-guide.jsp

© and ℗ 2010 Odyssey Productions, Inc. For the Estate of Alan Lomax

**Global Jukebox**

All songs Global Jukebox Publishing (BMI)

1. Young Bros.: Church, I Know We Got Another Building (Not Made with Hands)

2. Floyd Batts & prisoners: Dollar Mamie

3. Texas Gladden, Hobart Smith & Preston Smith: Lonely Tombs

4. Union Choir of the Church of God and Saints Of Christ: Didn't Old Pharaoh Get Lost

5. Almeda Riddle: Rainbow Mid Life's Willows

6. Fred McDowell: I'm Going Down That Gravel

7. Spencer Moore: The Girl I Left Behind

8. Vera Ward Hall: Riding in a Buggy/ Candy Gal

9. Wade Ward: Cumberland Gap

10. Bessie Jones & group: Reg'lar, Reg'lar, Rolling Under

11. I. D. Back: Poor Pilgrim of Sorrow

12. Miles & Bob Pratcher: I'm Gonna Live Anyhow Until I Die

# Track Notes

**01. *Church, I Know We Got Another Building (Not Made with Hands)***

Ed Young, fife; Lonnie Young Sr., bass drum; G. D. Young, snare drum. Como, Mississippi. September 21, 1959.

In 1942, during a joint research project of the Library of Congress and Nashville's Fisk University, Alan Lomax made the first-ever recordings of the fife and drum music of the Mississippi Hill Country, east of the Delta. "Finding this music still alive," he later wrote, "was the greatest surprise of all my collecting trips in America." Played now exclusively for entertainment at country picnics and dances, its roots stretch to before the Revolutionary War, when black fife and drum corps accompanied local militias — one of Thomas Jefferson's slaves is said to have played in such a corps. Their music is considered to be one of the oldest extant forms of African music in North America. Lomax recalled in 1993: "Watching the Young brothers' line of fife and drums sashay across the yard, enclosed by their dancing family, I saw in my mind's eye the jazz parades of New Orleans. . . . I remembered the Mardi Gras parades in Trinidad and Rio and the wild *rara* parades of Haiti and the films I'd seen of African processionals, and I could see that this family party in northern Mississippi belonged to that African tradition." Sacred pieces have seldom been recorded by fife and drum ensembles; this one is widespread in the black congregational repertoire. The Young brothers' band was later christened the Southern Fife and Drum Corps and appeared at the Newport Folk Festival and a Friends of Old-Time Music concert in the 1960s.

## 02.  *Dollar Mamie*

Floyd Batts and prisoners, vocals
and axes. Camp 11, Parchman Farm
(Mississippi State Penitentiary), Parchman, Mississippi. September 16, 1959.

Alan Lomax first experienced the group work
songs of Southern black prisoners in 1933,
when he was seventeen years old. He and his
father John A. Lomax visited penitentiaries that
year in Texas, Louisiana, Tennessee, and
Mississippi, making the first audio recordings of
a music remarkable for its intensity, creativity,
and nobility in spite of the brutal conditions in
which it was spawned. The Lomaxes were
initially interested in the remote, insulated
prison farms as potential repositories of ante-
bellum black song; as Alan Lomax, Bruce
Jackson, and others have noted, they were for
all intents and purposes twentieth-century repli-
cas of the slave plantation, with unpaid black
laborers working under the whip and the gun.
But what the Lomaxes found there was nothing
less than a new music. The work songs adapted
the field holler — the free-metered, unaccompa-
nied solo song of protest and complaint that
sired the blues — into many-voiced chants
propelled by the rhythmic striking of axes and
hoes, and whose purpose was, as Jackson has
put it, "making it in Hell."

The Lomaxes returned to Angola (Louisiana) and
Parchman Farm in 1934 for further recordings,
and Alan made three more trips to Parchman
alone in 1947, 1948, and 1959. "In the pen
itself," Lomax wrote in 1957, "we saw that the
songs, quite literally, kept the men alive and
normal." They came "out of the filthy darkness
of the pen, touched with exquisite musicality . . .
a testimony to the love of truth and beauty
which is a universal human trait." But when he
made his last visit in 1959, Shirley Collins
remembers, Alan found that "the music had lost
something of its grandeur and despair. It may
have been that conditions, although still harsh,

were not as brutal as they had been, or perhaps
it was that the younger prisoners didn't want to
keep up the old way of singing and the old
songs." This performance — featuring the characters of Dollar Mamie and Dollar Bob, and
recorded in some form by the Lomaxes at every
one of their Parchman sessions — might have
struck Alan this way, what with its laughter and
falsetto asides. But as a prisoner from Texas's
Ramsey State Farm told Bruce Jackson:
"Sometimes a guy be burdened down and he
don't want to pass his burden on to nobody.
That's because he don't want nobody feeling
sorry for him or thinking he's feeling sorry for
hisself. So he do it in a song, and he'd make it
real sad. . . . Well, he's thinking about his family
and doesn't want the other people to know it so
he makes it into a joke song, a work song."
When Jackson made his last recordings in the
Texas prison farm system in 1966, the mecha-
nization of prison agriculture was pushing the
work songs into obsolescence. By the early
1970s, they had become extinct.

## 03.  *Lonely Tombs*

Texas Gladden, vocal; Hobart Smith,
vocal and guitar; Preston Smith, vocal.
Bluefield, Virginia. August 24, 1959.

Over a dozen years had passed since Alan
Lomax had last seen the talented multi-instrumentalist Hobart Smith and his gifted ballad-
singing sister, Texas Gladden. In 1946 the
siblings had left their homes in southwest
Virginia's Blue Ridge for a trip to New York, a
concert with Jean Ritchie at Columbia University, and a session at Decca Studios, where
Lomax was then serving as a producer of an
American folk-music album series. Alan's first
stop in 1959 was to visit the Smith family,
although he found that failing health had somewhat constricted the abilities Texas had demon-
strated in '46 and earlier, in 1941, when he first
recorded her. (Lomax returned in 1942 to record
Hobart Smith, as Texas had told him that "I've

got a brother who can play anything.") Hobart, on the other hand, was as spry as ever — on guitar, fiddle, banjo, even piano. Preston Smith was Hobart and Texas's brother and a Pentecostal Holiness preacher; he joined them for this nineteenth-century Baptist hymn they had learned from their mother. By 1959, it had become a popular country gospel number recorded by the likes of Wade Mainer, the Stanley Brothers, and Hank Williams.

### 04. *Didn't Old Pharaoh Get Lost*

Caleb Garris, lead vocal, with the Union Choir of the Church of God and Saints of Christ. Belleville, Virginia. April 30, 1960.

The Church of God and Saints of Christ was founded in 1896 by Prophet William Saunders Crowdy, who taught that African Americans are the true descendants of the Ten Tribes of Israel. Its members, often called the Black Hebrews or Black Israelites, observe the holidays of the Jewish calendar, keep the Sabbath, and wear yarmulkes; they also use elements of Christian ritual, like immersion baptism. The First Tabernacle of the COGASOC, located in Belleville, Virginia, outside of Suffolk, is home to an a cappella choir with a repertoire of unique spirituals, drawn from the Hebrew Bible and composed especially for use in the Church. "I myself have heard no group," Lomax wrote in 1960, that "combines in such an engaging way a repertoire of fresh and thoroughly inspired songs, a conventional choral technique, and which at the same time has not lost the rhapsodic, swinging style [that] ennobles and enlivens American Negro folk music." The Church describes its songs as being "borne of the personal and spiritual experience of their authors and also reflect the doctrine and history of our Organization. The lyrics are often taken directly from scripture and enwrapped in engaging melodies." This performance is a medley of three classic African American spirituals:

"Didn't Old Pharaoh Get Lost," "Rock of Ages," and "None But the Righteous."

### 05. *Rainbow Mid Life's Willows*

Almeda Riddle, vocal. Greers Ferry, Arkansas. Early October, 1959.

For decades one of America's foremost traditional singers was Almeda "Granny" Riddle of Cleburne County, Arkansas, renowned for her singing
and her song collecting. Although tornados — a common scourge of northwestern Arkansas — had killed her husband and son, destroyed her home, and wiped out her treasured handwritten collection of ballads, she was still dedicated to seeking out and preserving the old songs.
"Rainbow Mid Life's Willows," the macabre tale of a young woman imprisoned by her family to keep her from her lover, is also known in America as "Locks and Bolts," and it is descended from a British broadsheet published in 1631 as "The Constant Lover." Riddle discovered the text in a notebook kept by a girl who had been dead for over forty years; it was stored away among her effects in the girl's grandmother's attic. When Almeda brought it home, she found that her father could recall its first and last verses, as well as its tune, which she sings here. Granny Riddle became a fixture on the folk-festival circuit from the mid-1960s through the early '80s, and she made a number of albums reflecting her huge repertoire of ballads, lyric songs, children's material, and hymns. She died in 1986.

### 06. *I'm Going Down That Gravel*

Fred McDowell, vocal and guitar; Fanny Davis, comb; Miles Pratcher, guitar. Como, Mississippi. September 22, 1959.

Fred McDowell was a farmer who emerged from the woods on the first day of fall, 1959, and ambled over to his neighbor Lonnie Young's front porch in his overalls with a guitar in hand. Lomax had no idea what he was in for, but after

McDowell's first song he knew he was in the presence of one of the most original, talented, and affecting country bluesmen ever recorded.

After McDowell performed several of his solo blues, accompanying himself on guitar and bottleneck slide, he was joined by his neighbor Miles Pratcher on second guitar and his sister Fanny Davis on "kazoo." Lomax recalled Davis "singing along through a comb, her man's felt hat falling over one eye, her plaits sticking out every which way, her legs wide apart, leaning her big body in toward Fred and mixing her notes with his." Davis was also a singer at the Hunter's Chapel in Como, and in 1966 she provided the lead vocal on Fred's first recorded version of "You Got to Move," which the Rolling Stones later made, for better or worse, into their signature song.

Fred's "I'm Going Down That Gravel" (also called "Gravel Road Blues") borrows some of its tune and its first two verses from Sleepy John Estes's "The Girl I Love, She Got Long Curly Hair" (1929), replacing Estes's "I'm going to Brownsville" with "I'm going down that gravel." This recording has previously been issued under the erroneous titles of "Going Down to the Races" and "Going Down the River."

## 07. *The Girl I Left Behind*

Spencer Moore, vocal and guitar;
Roy Everett Blevins, mandolin.
Chilhowie, Virginia. September 3, 1959.

When Lomax visited him in 1959, Raymond Spencer Moore was farming tobacco on his small acreage in southwestern Virginia. "A family man," Alan wrote of him later. "Hospitable, slow-spoken, and as genuine as a rail fence." Although Lomax made only four recordings of him, Spencer has been said to know over five hundred songs — including blues, hokum, minstrel material, play-party ditties, contemporary country compositions, and a few topical pieces of his own devising. He also had quite a repertoire of ballads of

recent vintage and regional application (such as "The Lawson Family Murders"), as well as this Americanized variant of a widely sung (and oft-parodied) item, first published in Dublin at least as early as 1806.

As a child in Laurel Bloomery, Tennessee, Spencer was bounced on the knee of legendary fiddler G. B. Grayson, who would stop by to visit with Spencer's father, James Moore, himself a fiddler and banjo player. In the late '30s, Spence and his brother Joe organized a close-harmony duet in the style of the Blue Sky Boys and the Delmore Brothers, appearing at dances and tent shows as far away as New York and Pennsylvania, and on one occasion sharing the stage with the Carter Family. After service in World War II, Spencer and his wife settled near Chilhowie, where he continued to farm and play music with his brother, friends, and neighbors for many decades. He died in 2011 at the age of 92.

## 08. *Riding in a Buggy/Candy Gal*

Vera Ward Hall, vocal. Livingston, Alabama. October 10, 1959.

Adele "Vera" Ward Hall (1902–1964), who worked all of her life as a washerwoman, nurse-maid, and cook, was regarded by the Lomaxes as one of America's greatest singers. She first came to the attention of John A. Lomax in 1937, when Ruby Pickens Tartt, folklorist and chair of the Federal Writers' Project of Sumter County, Alabama, introduced them. Lomax recorded Hall during three separate sessions in 1937, 1939, and 1940, writing that she had "the loveliest voice I have ever recorded." She sang Baptist hymns with her cousin Dock Reed and other Livingston friends, but she was also willing to record blues, ballads, and "worldly songs" such as "Stagolee," "John Henry," and "Boll Weevil," learned from her friend Rich Amerson, and forbidden by her family.

Alan Lomax met Hall in 1948, when he arranged for her and Reed to come to New York City for an American Music Festival. Their time together resulted in six and a half hours of recordings and the raw material for her oral biography, which Lomax published in *The Rainbow Sign* (1959). In that book Vera is called "Nora" to protect her identity and honor her confidences.

Making his first trip to Vera's home in Livingston, Alan found her voice and her eagerness to sing undiminished. Simple as they are, these brief ring-play verses nonetheless exemplify the delicacy and pathos of her ability. Five years later Lomax wrote in her obituary in *Sing Out!*: "The sound comes from deep within her when she sings, from a source of gold and light, otherwise hidden, and falls directly upon your ear like sunlight. … It is from singers like Vera Hall that all of us who love folk music in America have everything to learn. Her performances were all graced with dignity and love."

## 09. *Cumberland Gap*

Wade Ward, banjo. Galax, Virginia. August 31, 1959.

Uncle Wade Ward (1892–1971) was the scion of a musical family whose roots in southwestern Virginia went back generations. He learned to pick the banjo at eleven and play the fiddle at sixteen; by the time he was eighteen he and his older brother Davy Crockett Ward were playing as a duo popular at dances, house raisings, and other social functions around their home in Independence, Virginia. Wade recorded commercially, both solo and with his Buck Mountain Band, for the OKeh label in the 1920s. Alan Lomax's father, John A. Lomax, recorded him in 1937 with Crockett's string band, the Bogtrotters, and solo on fiddle and banjo, before Alan and Pete Seeger met him at the 1939 Galax Fiddlers Convention. Another session in 1941 brought the total number of Library of Congress records featuring Ward to nearly two hundred—one of which was a version of "Cumberland Gap"—but Alan wanted his virtuosic banjo playing represented in the

Southern Journey recordings. Lomax wrote soon after of Uncle Wade: "He had a good few drinks in his time and played a few dances, and all of this mellowed him till he became as kindly and gentle as the green hills among which he spent his life. When he plays, you realize that the real secret of musicianship lies, not in the number of notes per second or in difficult passages mastered or in surprises or in great ideas, but in the message that each note carries."

## 10. *Reg'lar, Reg'lar, Rolling Under*

Bessie Jones, lead vocal, with Nat Rahmings, drum; Hobart Smith, banjo; Ed Young, fife; and John Davis, Henry Morrison, Albert Ramsay, and Emma Ramsay, vocals. Williamsburg, Virginia. April 28, 1960.

Lomax's Southern Journey field recording trip ended in October of 1959, but by April of the next year Alan was back recording in the South, this time in the capacity of music supervisor to the Colonial Williamsburg Foundation's film *Music of Williamsburg*. The aim was to re-create the sound of African American music as it might have been heard in Colonial Williamsburg, and, according to a strikingly progressive 1962 press release from the foundation, "to portray the important contributions of the Negro race to the nation's heritage." Lomax assembled a novel cast, comprised of many musicians he'd recorded several months earlier, and drawn from disparate locales. Ed Young came north from Como, Mississippi, to provide the necessary fife-blowing. Hobart Smith traveled east from Saltville, Virginia, in the Blue Ridge Mountains, with his four-string banjo and a clawhammer technique learned, in part, from an African American. Nat Rahmings, a Bahamian drummer and drum maker, was brought in from Miami. And the Georgia Sea Island Singers were the vocal group at the ensemble's core. After filming was completed, Lomax wrote, the "musicians stayed on for what turned out to be a day of extraordinary music-making and musical cross-fertilization." Alan had turned up this tune years before, having gone looking for the oldest published black dance songs in Virginia — its references to the drinking gourd evince its slavery-time origin — and he taught it to the group. "I cannot swear to the authenticity of this reconstructed material," Lomax continued. "But the musically conservative Sea Island singers gave it their enthusiastic approval." The foundation approved of it too, and featured it in the film.

### 11. *Poor Pilgrim of Sorrow*

Elder I. D. Back, vocal. Mount Olivet Old Regular Baptist Church, Blackey, Kentucky. September 5, 1959.

The somber lined-out hymnody of the Old Regular Baptists — in which a leader "lines out" a verse for the congregants to sing back, in their own fashion and their own time — takes a very different approach to congregational singing than that, say, of the Sacred Harp. And unlike Sacred Harp singing, which is currently enjoying a remarkable upsurge of interest, the lining hymns are a rare holdover of a once-widespread singing style that is only getting rarer. Dating to the middle of the seventeenth century, lining was practiced throughout the British Isles and New England, but by 1959 they were being sung in just a handful of remote locales: in Presbyterian churches of the Gaelic Isles of Scotland; among some African American Baptist (and, occasionally, Methodist) churches in the deep South; and in the Old Regular Baptist meetinghouses of the central Appalachians. Elder Back here performs a solo version of "Poor Pilgrim of Sorrow," usually lined out at Old Regular Baptist meetings.

Alan Lomax read the melancholy texts of hymns like this one as reflections of the early American Revivalists' lonely struggles for survival and salvation on the frontier. "The authority of the established church was broken" upon coming

to America, Lomax remarked in 1982, and the pioneers found that now "every man had his own personal relationship to God, to heaven, to morality — he was responsible for himself. And Americans took this burden first. This was what made their faces so flinty. This is why they had to have such a strong and rigid morality. That's what made it possible for them to go as individuals and in small groups across the Appalachians into the unknown, and survive as human beings."

> *I am a poor pilgrim of sorrow,*
> *Cast out in this wide world to roam;*
> *I have no promise of tomorrow,*
> *I've started to make heaven my home.*

### 12. *I'm Gonna Live Anyhow Until I Die*

Miles Pratcher, vocal and guitar; Bob Pratcher, fiddle. Como, Mississippi. September 22, 1959.

The Pratcher brothers were neighbors of Fred McDowell in Como, and also farmers, but were of an earlier musical generation. Miles and Bob were repositories of the raggy country dance music that would have been heard at picnics and other social occasions in the turn-of-the-century Mississippi Hill Country. Lomax wrote of this performance in 1978 that he "always thought of this genre as a bluesy ballad in ragtime," lying chronologically and stylistically "between black square dance music and the first true instrumental blues." "I'm Going to Live Anyhow Until I Die" was composed in 1901 by the black rag writer Shepard N. Edmonds, for whom it was a huge hit, and it found a renewed popularity in the 1920s as "Tennessee Coon" or "Coon from Tennessee" — about a wicked fellow who "never believed in church or Sunday school" — for hillbilly performers Charlie Poole, the Georgia Crackers, and the Georgia Yellow Hammers. In the hands of the Pratchers, Lomax wrote, "the blues are still happy. The Pratchers grinned bawdily through all their performances."

# Southern Journey Discography

*They no doubt meant it when they sang: "I'm gonna shake it well for my Lord."*

As soon as the Southern Journey was completed in spring 1960, Alan Lomax edited and Atlantic Records released (1960) seven LPs of recordings from the trip. The LPs were individually titled (Atlantic SD-1346 to 1352) and known collectively as the *Southern Folk Heritage Series*, and within a year Atlantic reissued the LPs as a set (Atlantic SD-HS 1, 1346-1352). In 1993 Atlantic released the same collection, reordered, as a four-CD set titled *Sounds of the South* (Atlantic 7 82496-2). The original LP titles are:

"Volume 1: Sounds of the South," *Southern Folk Heritage Series* (Atlantic SD-1346), 1960.

"Volume 2: Blue Ridge Mountain Music," *Southern Folk Heritage Series* (Atlantic SD-1347), 1960.

"Volume 3: Roots of the Blues," *Southern Folk Heritage Series* (Atlantic SD-1348), 1960.

"Volume 4: White Spirituals," *Southern Folk Heritage Series* (Atlantic SD-1349), 1960.

"Volume 5: American Folk Songs for Children," *Southern Folk Heritage Series* (Atlantic SD-1350), 1960.

"Volume 6: Negro Church Music," *Southern Folk Heritage Series* (Atlantic SD-1351), 1960.

"Volume 7: The Blues Roll On," *Southern Folk Heritage Series* (Atlantic SD-1352), 1960.

Additionally in 1960 Alan Lomax and his assistant Carla Rotolo edited the 12-LP *Southern Journey* series (25001-25012) for Prestige International Records under the following individual titles:

*Georgia Sea Islands, Southern Journey, Vol. 1* (Prestige International INT-25001), 1960.

*Georgia Sea Islands, Southern Journey, Vol. 2* (Prestige International INT-25002), 1960.

*Ballads and Breakdowns from the Southern Mountains, Southern Journey, Vol. 3* (Prestige International INT-25003), 1960.

*Banjo Songs, Ballads and Reels from the Southern Mountains, Southern Journey, Vol. 4* (Prestige International INT-25004), 1960.

*Deep South...Sacred and Sinful, Southern Journey, Vol. 5* (Prestige International INT-25005), 1960.

*Folk Songs from the Ozarks, Southern Journey, Vol. 6* (Prestige International INT-25006), 1960.

*All Day Singing from "The Sacred Harp," Southern Journey, Vol. 7* (Prestige International INT-25007), 1960.

*The Eastern Shores, Southern Journey, Vol. 8* (Prestige International INT-25008), 1960.

*Bad Man Ballads, Southern Journey, Vol. 9* (Prestige International INT-25009), 1960.

*Yazoo Delta Blues and Spirituals, Southern Journey, Vol. 10* (Prestige International INT-25010), 1960.

*Southern White Spirituals, Southern Journey, Vol. 11* (Prestige International INT-25011), 1960.

*Honor the Lamb: The Belleville A Cappella Choir of the Church of God and Saints in Christ, Southern Journey, Vol. 12* (Prestige International 25012), 1960.

In 1977, New World Records released four LPs, part of its *Recorded Anthology of American Music* series, derived primarily from the Prestige International LP set.

*White Spirituals from The Sacred Harp: The Alabama Sacred Harp Convention* (New World NW 205), 1977.
*Roots of the Blues* (New World 252), 1977.
*Georgia Sea Island Songs* (New World NW 278), 1977.
*The Gospel Ship: Baptist Hymns and White Spirituals from the Southern Mountains* (New World NW 294), 1977.

The Prestige International LPs were revised and expanded to 13 volumes by Matthew Barton, Andrew L. Kaye, and Anna Lomax Wood of Alan's Association for Cultural Equity and released by Rounder Records in 1997. The new titles were:

*Southern Journey, Vol. 1: Voices from the American South: Blues, ballads, hymns, reels, shouts, chanteys and work songs* (Rounder CD 1701), 1997.
*Southern Journey, Vol. 2: Ballads & Breakdowns: Songs from the Southern Mountains* (Rounder CD 1702), 1997.
*Southern Journey, Vol. 3: 61 Highway Mississippi: Delta Country Blues, Spirituals, Work Songs & Dance Music* (Rounder CD 1703), 1997.
*Southern Journey, Vol. 4: Brethren, We Meet Again: Southern White Spirituals* (Rounder CD 1704), 1997.
*Southern Journey, Vol. 5: Bad Man Ballads: Songs of Outlaws and Desperadoes* (Rounder CD 1705), 1997.

*Southern Journey, Vol. 6: Sheep, Sheep Don'tcha Know the Road: Southern Music, Sacred and Sinful* (Rounder CD 1706), 1997.
*Southern Journey, Vol. 7: Ozark Frontier: Ballads and Old-timey Music from Arkansas* (Rounder CD 1707), 1997.
*Southern Journey, Vol. 8: Velvet Voices: Eastern Shores Choirs, Quartets, and Colonial Era Music* (Rounder CD 1708), 1997.
*Southern Journey, Vol. 9: Harp of a Thousand Strings: All Day Singing from The Sacred Harp* (Rounder CD 1709), 1997.
*Southern Journey, Vol. 10: And Glory Shone Around: More All Day Singing from The Sacred Harp* (Rounder CD 1710), 1997.
*Southern Journey, Vol. 11: Honor the Lamb: The Belleville A Cappella Choir* (Rounder CD 1711), 1997.
*Southern Journey, Vol. 12: Georgia Sea Islands: Biblical Songs and Spirituals* (Rounder CD 1712), 1997.
*Southern Journey, Vol. 13: Earliest Times: Georgia Sea Islands Songs for Everyday Living* (Rounder CD 1713), 1997.

Additionally, as part of their *Alan Lomax Collection*, the Association for Cultural Equity and Rounder Records issued material from the Southern Journey on the following CDs:

*Alan Lomax Collection Sampler* (Rounder CD 1700), 1997.
*Fred McDowell: The First Recordings* (Rounder CD 1718), 1997.
*Songs of Christmas from the Alan Lomax Collection* (Rounder CD 1719), 1998.
*Hobart Smith: Blue Ridge Legacy* (Rounder CD 1799), 2001.
*Texas Gladden: Ballad Legacy* (Rounder CD 1800), 2001.

*The Land Where the Blues Began* (Rounder CD 1861), 2002.

*Alan Lomax: Popular Songbook* (Rounder CD 1863), 2003.

*Alan Lomax: Blues Songbook* (Rounder CD 1866), 2003.

The 1959 performance of "Po' Lazarus" by James Carter and group was issued on the soundtrack to the film *O Brother, Where Art Thou?* (Lost Highway), 2000.

Most recently, in 2010–2011, seven volumes commemorating the fiftieth anniversary of the Southern Journey were edited by Nathan Salsburg and released on LP by Mississippi Records and as digital downloads by the Alan Lomax Archive's Global Jukebox imprint. The titles are:

*Wave the Ocean, Wave the Sea: Field Recordings from Alan Lomax's Southern Journey, 1959–1960* (Mississippi Records MR 57), 2010 (Global Jukebox GJ1001), 2010.

*Worried Now, Won't Be Worried Long: Field Recordings from Alan Lomax's Southern Journey, 1959–1960* (Mississippi Records MR 58), 2010 (Global Jukebox GJ1002), 2010.

*I'll Meet You on That Other Shore: Field Recordings from Alan Lomax's Southern Journey, 1959–1960* (Mississippi Records MR 59), 2010 (Global Jukebox GJ1003), 2010.

*I'll Be So Glad When the Sun Goes Down: Field Recordings from Alan Lomax's Southern Journey, 1959–1960* (Mississippi Records MR 60), 2010 (Global Jukebox GJ1004), 2011.

*I'm Gonna Live Anyhow Until I Die: Field Recordings from Alan Lomax's Southern Journey, 1959–1960* (Mississippi Records MR 65 [sic]), 2010 (Global Jukebox GJ1005), 2011.

*Fred McDowell: The Alan Lomax Recordings: Field Recordings from Alan Lomax's Southern Journey, 1959–1960* (Mississippi Records MR 72), 2011 (Global Jukebox GJ1007), 2011.

*Georgia Sea Island Singers: Join the Band* (Mississippi Records MRP-003), 2011 (Global Jukebox GJ1008), 2011.

# Image Credits

Except where otherwise credited, photographs are by Alan Lomax and are published courtesy of the Alan Lomax Archive (www.culturalequity.org).

The physical negatives and prints of the photographs reside in the collections of the American Folklife Center, Library of Congress, unless otherwise noted. If you would like to order reproductions of any of the photographs in this book, please visit the Library's Duplication Services website at www.loc.gov/duplicationservices.

COVER   afc2004004:01.01.0268

BACK C.   afc2004004:01.01.0056, photo by Shirley Collins

TITLE P.   afc2004004:01.01.0129

9   afc2004004:01.01.0066, photo by Shirley Collins

15   afc2004004:01.01.0231

20   Lomax with camera, photo by Bill Ferris, William R. Ferris Collection, Southern Folklife Collection, Wilson Library, University of North Carolina at Chapel Hill

21   afc2004004:01.01.0284, photo by Shirley Collins

24   LC-USZ62-91680, Prints & Photographs Division, Library of Congress (public domain)

25   LC-USZ62-71616, Prints & Photographs Division, Library of Congress (public domain)

27   LC-USZ62-56331, photograph by Ruby Terrill Lomax, Prints & Photographs Division, Library of Congress

29   LC-USZ62-23008, Prints & Photographs Division, Library of Congress (public domain)

31   LC-USZ62-115667, Prints & Photographs Division, Library of Congress (public domain)

32   LC-USZ6-1723, Prints & Photographs Division, Library of Congress (public domain)

34   LC-USZ6-2237, Prints & Photographs Division, Library of Congress (public domain)

35   LC-USZ62-120995, photographer undocumented, Prints & Photographs Division, Library of Congress

36   LC-USZ62-32438, CBS photographer, Prints & Photographs Division, Library of Congress

37   Scotland 1958, photographer undocumented

38   afc2004004:01.02.0352, photo by Jeannette Bell

45 (TOP)   Tape box T886, cover (public domain)

45 (BOT)   Tape box T886, inside cover (public domain)

46   LC-USZ62-36138, Prints & Photographs Division, Library of Congress (public domain)

47   LC-USZ62-51339, Prints & Photographs Division, Library of Congress (public domain)

50   LC-DIG-ppmsc-00332, Prints & Photographs Division, Library of Congress (public domain)

56   LC-USZ61-1348, Prints & Photographs Division, Library of Congress (public domain)

58   Southern Journey Car Equipment List

59   afc2004004:01.01.0003

60   afc2004004:01.01.0017

61 (TOP)   afc2004004:01.01.0067

61 (BOT)   afc2004004:01.01.0068

62 (TOP)   afc2004004:01.01.0070

62 (BOT)   afc2004004:01.01.0072

63 (TOP)   afc2004004:01.01.0077

63 (BOT)   afc2004004:01.01.0079

64 (TOP)   afc2004004:01.01.0030

64 (BOT)   afc2004004:01.01.0043

65   afc2004004:01.01.0082

66   afc2004004:01.01.0049

67   afc2004004:01.01.0056, photo by Shirley Collins

68 (TOP)   afc2004004:01.01.0035, photo by Shirley Collins

68 (BOT)   afc2004004:01.01.0039

69   afc2004004:01.01.0090

70   afc2004004:01.01.0083

71   afc2004004:01.01.0097

72   afc2004004:01.01.0100

73 (TOP)   afc2004004:01.01.0112

73 (BOT)   afc2004004:01.01.0106

74 (TOP)   afc2004004:01.01.0129

74 (BOT)   afc2004004:01.01.0137

75   afc2004004:01.01.0133

| 76 | afc2004004:01.01.0140 |
|---|---|
| 77 | afc2004004:01.01.0142 |
| 78 | afc2004004:01.01.0146 |
| 79 | afc2004004:01.01.0169 |
| 80 | afc2004004:01.01.0158 |
| 81 | afc2004004:01.01.0258 |
| 82 | afc2004004:01.01.0183 |
| 83 | afc2004004:01.01.0184 |
| 84 | afc2004004:01.01.0190 |
| 85 | afc2004004:01.01.0189 |
| 86 | afc2004004:01.01.0187 |
| 87 (TOP) | afc2004004:01.01.0242 |
| 87 (BOT) | afc2004004:01.01.0198 |
| 88 | afc2004004:01.01.0299 |
| 89 | afc2004004:01.01.0304 |
| 90 | afc2004004:01.01.0281 |
| 91 | afc2004004:01.01.0288, photo by Shirley Collins |
| 92 | afc2004004:01.01.0380 |
| 93 | afc2004004:01.01.0374 |
| 94 | afc2004004:01.01.0396 |
| 95 (TOP) | afc2004004:01.01.0337 |
| 95 (BOT) | afc2004004:01.01.0341 |
| 96 | afc2004004:01.01.0430 |
| 97 (L) | afc2004004:01.01.0436 |
| 97 (R) | afc2004004:01.01.0426 |
| 98 | afc2004004:01.01.0687 |
| 99 (TOP) | afc2004004:01.01.0458 |
| 99 (BOT) | afc2004004:01.01.0469 |
| 100 | afc2004004:01.01.0455 |
| 101 | afc2004004:01.01.0449 |
| 102 (TOP) | afc2004004:01.01.0425 |
| 102 (BOT) | afc2004004:01.01.0421 |
| 103 | afc2004004:01.01.0264 |
| 104 | afc2004004:01.01.0472 |
| 105 | afc2004004:01.01.0768 |
| 106 | afc2004004:01.01.0499 |
| 107 | afc2004004:01.01.0502 |
| 108 (TOP) | afc2004004:01.01.0503 |
| 108 (BOT) | afc2004004:01.01.0557 |
| 109 | afc2004004:01.01.0511 |
| 110 (TOP) | afc2004004:01.01.0493 |
| 110 (BOT) | afc2004004:01.01.0513 |
| 111 (TOP) | afc2004004:01.01.0517 |
| 111 (BOT) | afc2004004:01.01.0519 |
| 112 | afc2004004:01.01.0649 |
| 113 | afc2004004:01.01.0665 |
| 114 | afc2004004:01.01.0628 |
| 115 | afc2004004:01.01.0588 |
| 116 | afc2004004:01.01.0650 |
| 117 | afc2004004:01.01.0681 |
| 118 | afc2004004:01.01.0751 |
| 119 | afc2004004:01.01.0756 |

# *Index*

"*This was 1959 and I finally had German mikes and a Cadillac of a recorder and was doing stereo — the first stereo field recordings made in the South. You should hear the recordings — for me, a life's dream realized.*"

— ALAN LOMAX, 1993